ROCK GUITAR BOOK

LEARN TO PLAY FROM SCRATCH!

BY RICK CARDINALI

Wise Publications

London / New York / ...rid / Hong Kong / Tokyo

Hi, Rick here, welcome to my very own basic guitar book. Whether you're an absolute beginner, can already play a little, or used to play and want to get back into it, I'll help you master the guitar. We'll begin with the basics, to make sure you start in the right way, and before you know it you'll be playing along to the tracks I've created specially for this book.

Every time you see this logo ⊚, it means that there's a track on the CDs that you should use at that point. Have a listen to Track 1 on CD 1 to get a taste of what you're about to learn! Some of the tracks have more than one exercise on them. When you get to the songs (starting on page 17 with *Zap!*), you'll see that each song has two CD tracks. The first is played slowly, with a rhythm count, the second is the full track at full speed.

That's all you need to know for now, let's get started. I hope you have as much fun learning from this book as I did writing it!

Rick

CONTENTS

Italics denote songs

Italics denote songs

THE GUITAR

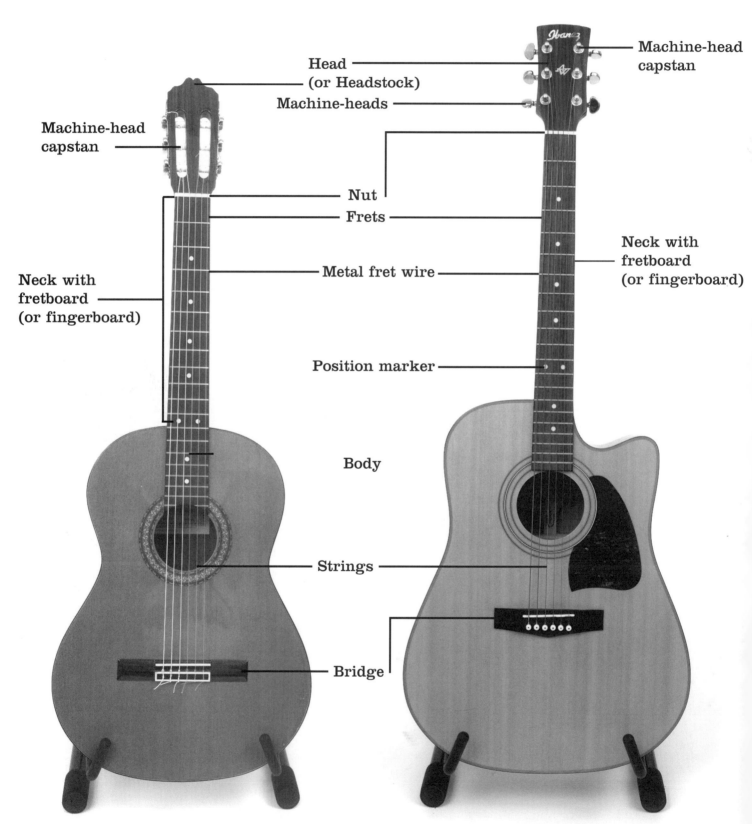

Head
(or Headstock)

Machine-heads

Machine-head
capstan

Machine-head
capstan

Nut

Frets

Neck with
fretboard
(or fingerboard)

Metal fret wire

Neck with
fretboard
(or fingerboard)

Position marker

Body

Strings

Bridge

Acoustic nylon-string guitar

Acoustic steel-string guitar

ELECTRIC GUITAR AND AMPLIFIER

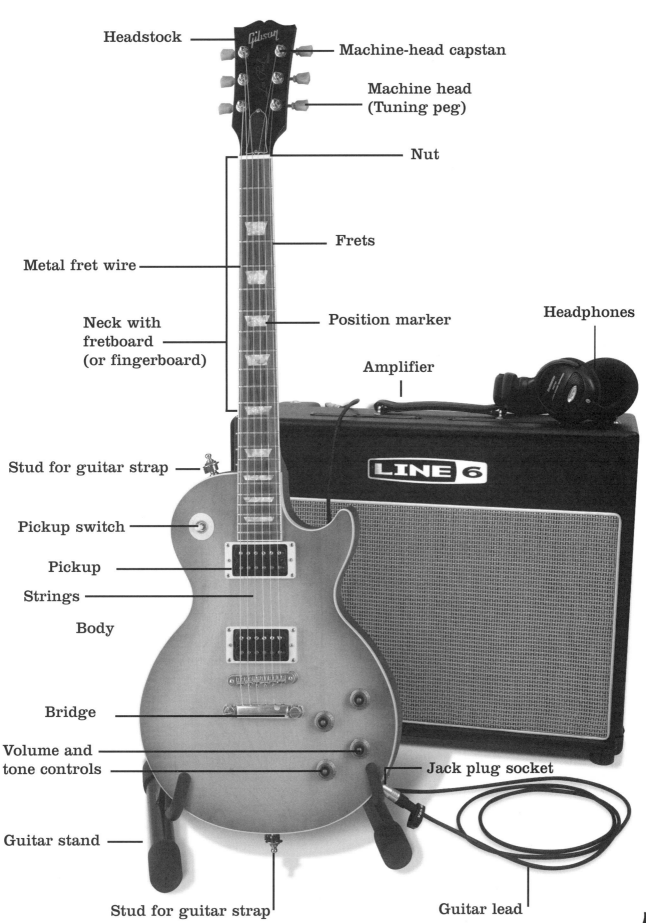

Headstock

Machine-head capstan

Machine head (Tuning peg)

Nut

Frets

Metal fret wire

Position marker

Headphones

Neck with fretboard (or fingerboard)

Amplifier

LINE 6

Stud for guitar strap

Pickup switch

Pickup

Strings

Body

Bridge

Volume and tone controls

Jack plug socket

Guitar stand

Stud for guitar strap

Guitar lead

STRINGS

Choosing strings is a matter of personal preference. However, the lighter the string's gauge the easier it is to press down against the fretboard. If you have an acoustic steel-string guitar, try using a set of **light-gauge** strings. These will be easy on your fingertips.

If you have a classical nylon-string guitar, **low-tension** strings will offer similar benefits. **Do not use steel strings on a guitar built for nylon strings, the tension could bend the neck or break the guitar. Nylon strings will not work on an electric guitar.**

SOME USEFUL ITEMS TO HAVE AT HAND

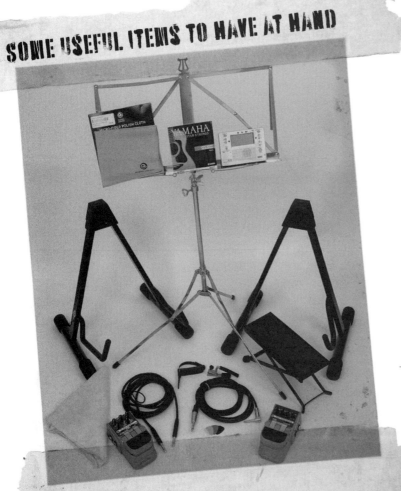

Keep a spare set of strings and plectrums in your guitar case. If you have an electric guitar, keep a spare guitar lead. Buy the best leads you can afford; a good lead will help minimise non-guitar noise from the amplifier and will be reliable. If you need to put your guitar down during a practice session, place it on a suitable guitar-stand. When you are storing your guitar, keep it in a hard-case. Guitars are available in many shapes and sizes so, if you do not have a guitar-stand or a hard-case, ask to have your guitar fitted for one at your local music shop. A programmable metronome will help you develop good timing.

CARE OF YOUR GUITAR

Polish the guitar and strings with a dry soft cloth before and after each practice session, this will help keep the guitar in good condition and extend the useful life of the strings.

CHANGING STRINGS

If you are not sure which type of string is suitable for your guitar, enquire at your local music shop. If you have difficulty changing the strings, ask if they may offer this service. When strings become old and worn, they start to sound dull and difficult to tune; you should change them well-before they reach this stage. As a minimum, try to change strings no less than once a year. A new set of strings can transform your guitar, they will sound bright and be satisfying to play.

POSTURE

Hold your guitar the way that feels most comfortable. Finding a comfortable posture helps to minimise strain and avoid back pain.

If you decide to stand, adjust your guitar strap to the length that will offer you the most convenient position for playing.

Wearing your guitar strap 'long' may enable you to strike classic Rock 'n' Roll poses but is unlikely to help you learn to play.

If you decide to sit, the ideal chair will allow you to sit in such a way that your femur (thigh bone) is horizontal and your feet are able to rest flat on the floor.

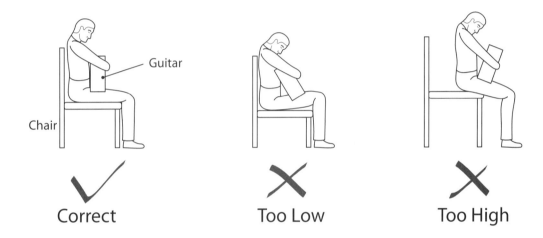

Correct   Too Low   Too High

Whichever posture you choose, rest your right arm (just below the elbow) lightly on the body of the guitar in such a way that your right hand is poised over the strings near the bridge.

THE RIGHT HAND

PLECTRUM STYLE

Plectrum style

Some guitarists use a plectrum (or pick) to 'strike' the strings. A plectrum is held between the thumb and index finger (as shown in the diagram). Experiment with different types, a flexible plectrum with a good grip is easiest to control while learning to play.

Plectrum down-strokes

In the first part of the book you will use your plectrum to strike the strings with a down-stroke (see diagram). A down-stroke should start on the upper side of the string and then proceed downwards (towards the floor).

Down-stroke

DOWN-STROKE

TUNING TO THE CD

⊙ **Tracks 2-8**

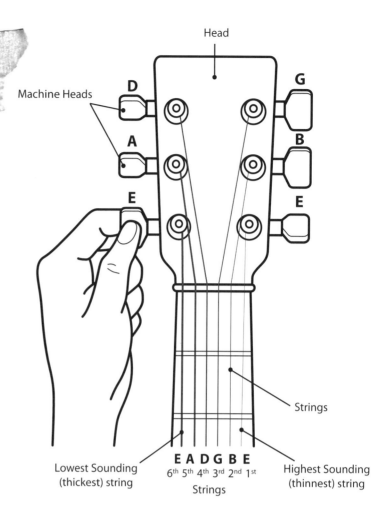

Head

Machine Heads

D   G
A   B
E   E

Strings

E A D G B E
6th 5th 4th 3rd 2nd 1st
Strings

Lowest Sounding
(thickest) string

Highest Sounding
(thinnest) string

Tune your guitar with the help of the tuning instructions on the CD. The tuning tone (or pitch) for each string is sounded separately. The letters adjacent to the machine-heads in the diagram show the note to which the attached string should be tuned. The strings are often referred to by their letter-note name as well as their string number (for example: B or 2nd string) so it makes sense to learn them both.

Tune each string to the correct pitch by winding the relevant machine-head up or down. Some alternative methods of tuning are shown towards the end of the book. Whichever method you decide to use, it is best to start with the thickest string, E or 6th and end with the thinnest, E or 1st. Check the tuning of your guitar regularly during each practice session.

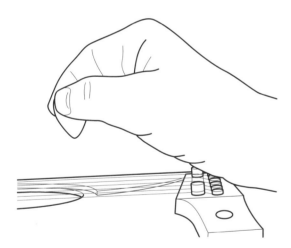

Right Hand Rest Position*

If you are having difficulty striking the strings accurately, try resting the side of your right hand lightly on the bridge of the guitar as shown in the diagram.

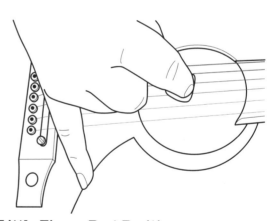

Little Finger Rest Position.

Alternatively try resting your little finger on the body of the guitar as shown in the diagram.

---

* Avoid touching the strings with the side of your hand or resting your hand too heavily as it may 'mute' the sound of the strings. The Right Hand Rest Position looks quite similar to an effect called Palm-Muting which is shown on page 49.

GUITAR TABLATURE

Tablature is read from left to right like handwriting and traditional music notation.

If you have difficulty relating the tablature numbers to your fretboard you could stick small self-adhesive pieces of paper, with the fret numbers on, along the neck of your guitar.

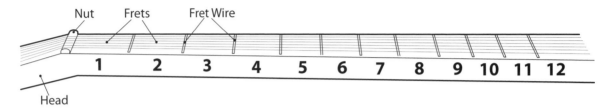

Guitar neck viewed from player's perspective

The Guitar Tablature stave

Many books of guitar music are written using a combination of traditional music notation and guitar tablature (often abbreviated to tab). The guitar tab stave has six lines, each representing a string on the guitar. Sometimes suggested fingerings are shown above the tab stave.

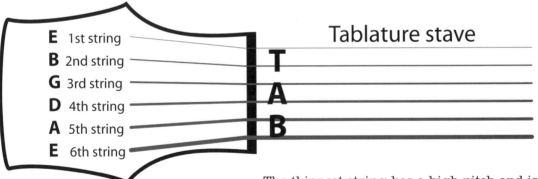

The thinnest string has a high pitch and is shown at the top of the stave. The thickest string has a low pitch and is shown at the bottom of the stave. All the lines (representing the strings) are shown with the same thickness on the tablature stave for ease of reading.

* You should not play the guitar with damp hands, damp skin tends to be more vulnerable to wear from the strings.
** To make the text easier to read, left-hand finger numbers will be spelt out thus: First; Second, Third and Fourth. Fret and String numbers will be shortened thus: 1st; 2nd; 3rd etc...

The fingers of your left hand are numbered as shown in the diagram. Most often you will use your:

First finger on the 1st fret.**
Second finger on the 2nd fret.
Third finger on the 3rd fret and
Fourth finger on the 4th fret.

The strings are held-down (or stopped) by pressing your left-hand fingertips against the fretboard as indicated.

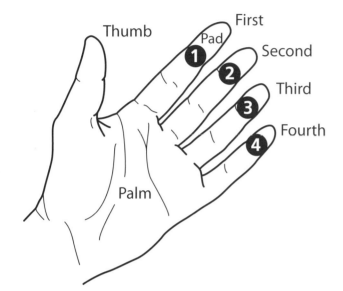

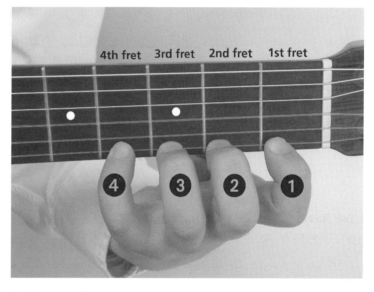

A number shown on a line indicates the fret on which your finger should be placed to hold-down (or 'stop') the string.

So **2** indicates the **2nd fret** and **3** indicates the **3rd fret** etc...

A zero (0) denotes that the string should be played open or unstopped.

In the following tab example you would place your third finger on the 3rd fret of the 1st string.

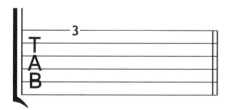

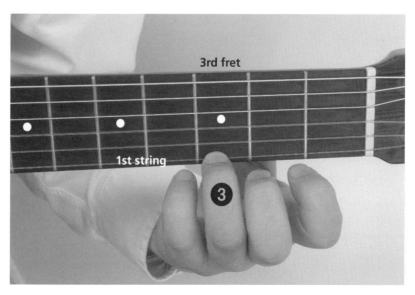

READING MUSIC

Music is written on a **stave** (or **staff**) which has five equally spaced parallel lines and four spaces. The symbol seen at the beginning of each stave in this book is called the **Treble Clef**. The Treble Clef encircles the line representing the note **G** on the stave (it looks like a rather stylish G).*

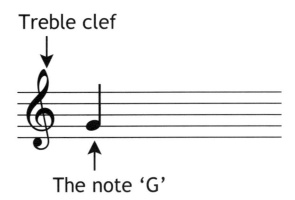

Treble clef

The note 'G'

Musical tones are represented by notes written on the stave. The **pitch** of a note describes how **high** or **low** it sounds. Notes are given the letter-names **A, B, C, D, E, F** and **G**.

The notes are written either on **lines** or in **spaces.**

A B C D E F G A B C D E F G A *etc.*

The notes on the lines are E, G, B, D and F and the notes in the spaces are F, A, C, E.

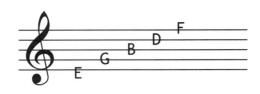

The mnemonic: **E**very **G**reat **B**and **D**eserves **F**ame is one way to remember the **lines**.

The word: **FACE** is an easy way to remember the **spaces**.

* The Treble clef fixes the note 'G' on the stave and is sometimes called the G clef. There are several different clefs but a stave is used for all of them.

RHYTHM

The stave is separated into **bars** (or measures) by vertical lines called barlines. Each bar has a fixed number of **beats** according to the **time signature** of the music.

A beat may be described as the natural foot-tapping rhythm of a piece of music. A **time signature** appears at the beginning of most music and consists of two numbers. The top number denotes the number of **beats** in each bar. The lower number denotes the **value of a beat**. For example: The time signature 4/4 (pronounced four, four) describes **four beats** in a bar, each beat with the **value of a quarter-note** (as shown below). The four quarter-notes add up to a **whole-note**. Most Rock and Pop pieces have four beats in a bar.

They are counted like this:

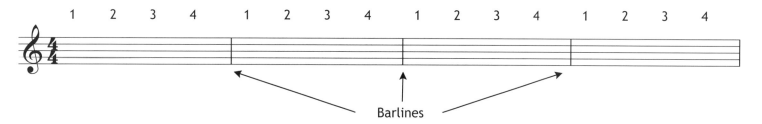

Barlines

Notes tell the musician what sound to play, when to play it, and how long the sound should last. Notes have a time-value that corresponds to the beat.

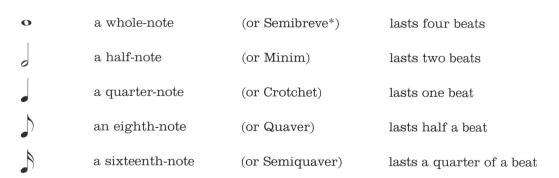

𝅝	a whole-note	(or Semibreve*)	lasts four beats
𝅗𝅥	a half-note	(or Minim)	lasts two beats
𝅘𝅥	a quarter-note	(or Crotchet)	lasts one beat
𝅘𝅥𝅮	an eighth-note	(or Quaver)	lasts half a beat
𝅘𝅥𝅯	a sixteenth-note	(or Semiquaver)	lasts a quarter of a beat

Eighth-notes are first used on page 34, sixteenth-notes are not used in this book, but it's useful to know about them.

A piece of music in 4/4 time may contain notes in any combination of time-value, provided the total time-value per bar adds up to one whole-note (semibreve).

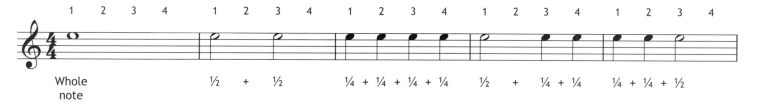

Whole note   ½ + ½   ¼ + ¼ + ¼ + ¼   ½ + ¼ + ¼   ¼ + ¼ + ½

The stems of the notes may point upwards or downwards depending on where the note is placed on the stave:

* The bracketed note names like Semibreve, Minim and Crotchet represent an alternative to the Whole-note, Half-note, Quarter-note naming system. It is recommended that you learn both names for each note.

Whether you are going to learn new notes, practise an exercise or play a piece that you already know, make sure that your guitar is always in tune.

Check the open strings of your guitar against the tuning tones found on CD 1 tracks 3 to 8.

Learning New Notes

Find the finger positions for the notes on your fretboard by following the music and tab. Read the traditional music notation while you play each note. Remember to strike only the string indicated. Check the sound of the note against the CD demonstration.

Say the letter-names out loud as you play them, this will help you to remember the relationship between:
– the position of the note on the stave
– its 'letter-name'
– its position on the fretboard
– the left-hand finger used to stop the string.

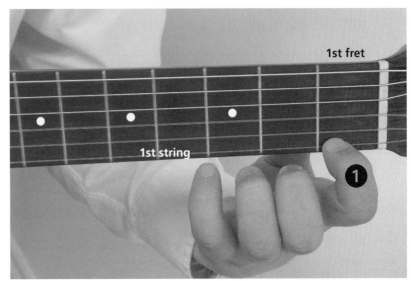

Your left-hand fingers should be held as near perpendicular to the fretboard as possible when holding down the strings. The fingernails of your left hand will need to be just short enough to avoid forcing your fingers into a less convenient posture.

Correct Finger Position

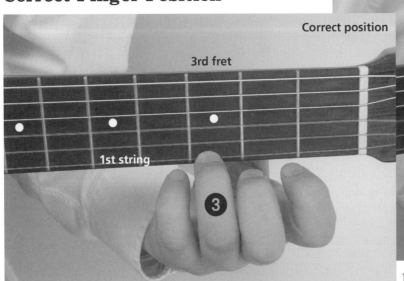

Playing close to the fret wire will produce a clear sound.

Incorrect Finger Position

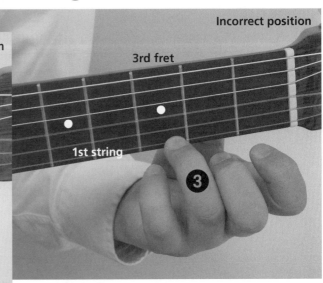

Playing towards the back of the fret may make the note 'buzz' or sound dull.

Learning and Practising a Piece of Music

Follow the traditional music notation for the piece you wish to learn while you listen to the slow practice track on the CD.

Take note of any repeat signs and any other items which are new to you. Then switch off the CD and play through the music slowly, using the guitar tab for reference. When you feel comfortable play-along with the slow practice track. Finally, play-along with the full-speed backing track.

Maintain a steady tempo (speed) throughout each practice attempt by using a metronome; this is important for the development of your timing. Avoid playing the easier parts quickly and then slowing down for the 'tricky bits'.

Select a slightly faster tempo at the start of each 'practice attempt' and stick to it.

Each time you practise passages that you find difficult, you are steadily improving your technique and removing obstacles to your success.

If, after a reasonable period of practice, you still find a passage too difficult to play, move on and come back to it later. You may just need a break!

If what you are playing sounds out of tune with the CD or unpleasant to the ear, turn to the Troubleshooting section on page 101.

Important

Guitar tab is shown in many books **alongside**, but **not as a substitute for**, traditional music notation. **Read the traditional music notation first and use the tab as a reference**. The approach used in this book will help you to relate musical notes seen on the traditional music stave to positions on the guitar fretboard (see page 117).*

*Now try the **Basics** section of the Quiz starting on page 102.*

* When learning more complex pieces, traditional music notation can be ambiguous with regard to the most convenient fretboard position. In these cases, guitar tab can be helpful.

Track 9

 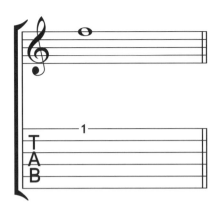 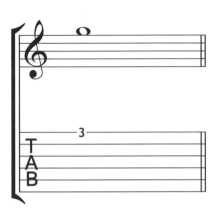

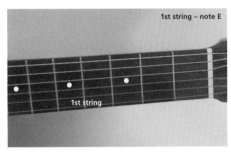

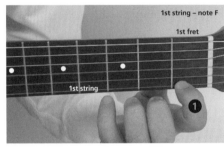

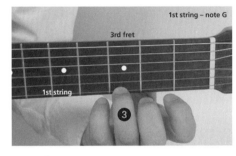

Note E
Open
1st string

Note F
First finger, 1st fret
1st string

Note G
Third finger, 3rd fret
1st string

Follow the procedure 'Learning New Notes' (shown on page 14).

Commit to memory, the position of each note on the stave; its letter-name; its fretboard position and the left-hand finger used to hold-down the string.*

Left-hand fingering is easy to remember at this stage. Unless otherwise indicated, use your:
first finger on the 1st fret
second finger on the 2nd fret
third finger on the 3rd fret
fourth finger on the 4th fret
Play all the notes with down-strokes (see page 8).

Check your tuning again, before trying the following exercise with the CD.

Track 10 *1st String Exercise*

This symbol is known as a 'final bar line'.
It denotes the end of a piece of music.

Count: 1 2 3 4 1 2 3 4 1 2 3 4 1 2 3 4 1 2 3 4

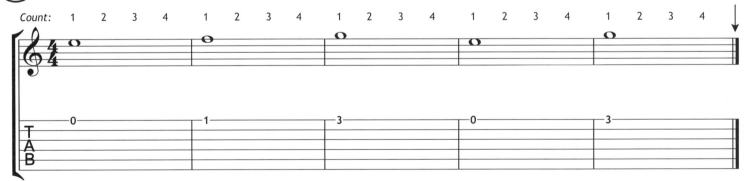

* Knowing the fret positions and the 'letter-names' of the notes (off by heart) will help you to understand the relationship between notes, scales and chords later on.

With just these first three notes you are now ready to try the following tunes:

Track 11-12 *Zap!*

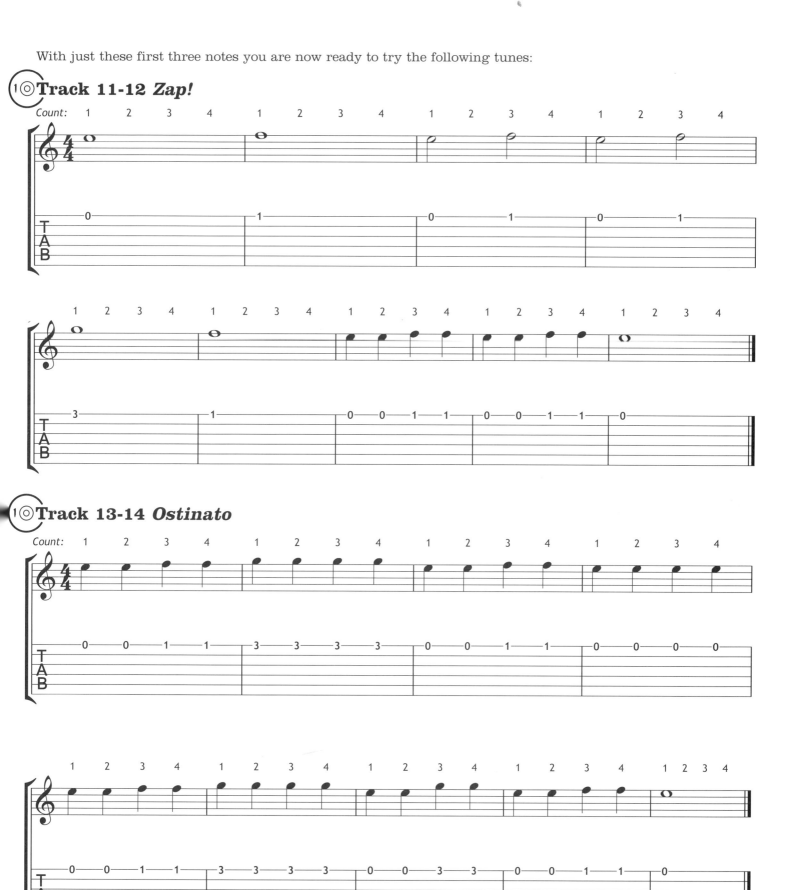

Track 13-14 *Ostinato*

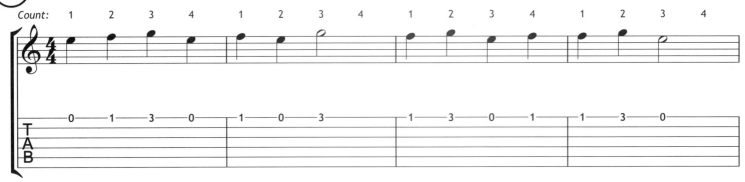

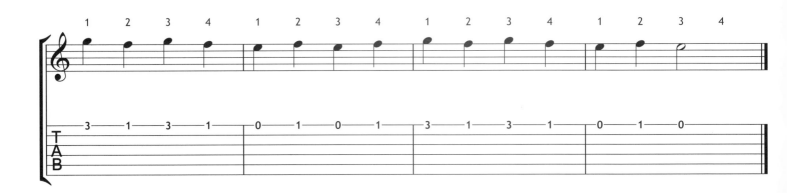

Dotted Notes

A dot placed to the right of a note increases its time-value (or length) by half.*

For example the minim (or half-note) at the start of bar 1 is dotted. A minim lasts for two beats, the dot increases it by half the original value, which makes a total of three beats.

Track 17-18 *Sesquipedalia*

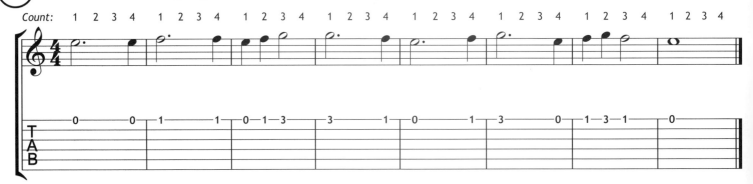

*Now try the **1st String** section of the Quiz on page 106.*

* The relationship between the time-value of notes and the beat is shown in the section entitled 'Rhythm' on page 13.

The song: 'Late, Late Spooky Show' provides a review of the notation and techniques you have learned so far. In particular, look out for the dotted minim in bar 4.

Track 19-20 *Late, Late Spooky Show*

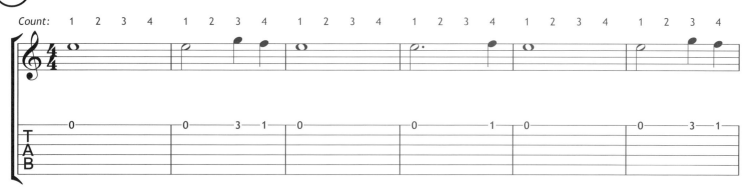

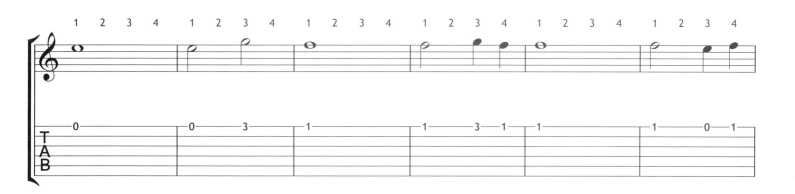

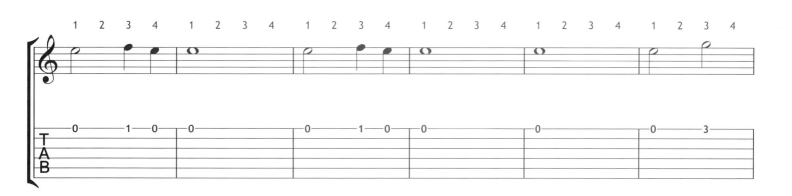

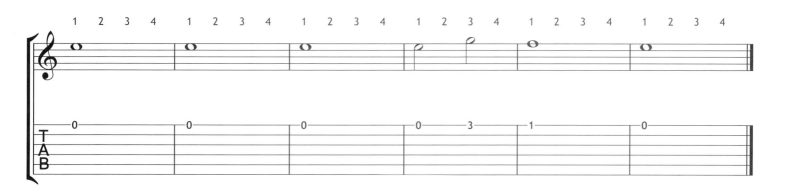

Track 21

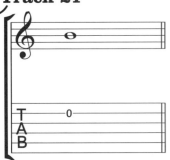

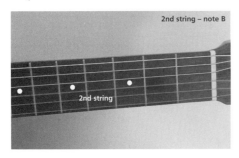

2nd string – note B

Note B
Open
2nd string

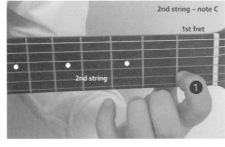

2nd string – note C
1st fret

Note C
First finger, 1st fret
2nd string

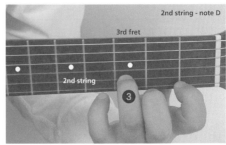

2nd string - note D
3rd fret

Note D
Third finger, 3rd fret
2nd string

Track 22 *2nd String Exercise*

Count: 1 2 3 4 1 2 3 4 1 2 3 4 1 2 3 4 1 2 3 4

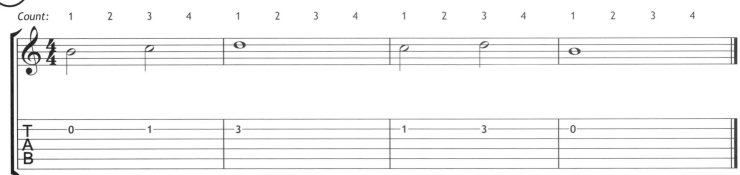

Track 23-24 *Repeat Signs*

These are repeat signs:

The music shown between these symbols should be repeated (i.e. played twice through). If the left-hand symbol does not appear the player should go back to the beginning of the piece.

Repeat Signs

Play twice through

Count: 1 2 3 4 1 2 3 4 1 2 3 4 1 2 3 4 1 2 3 4 1 2 3 4 1 2 3 4 1 2 3 4

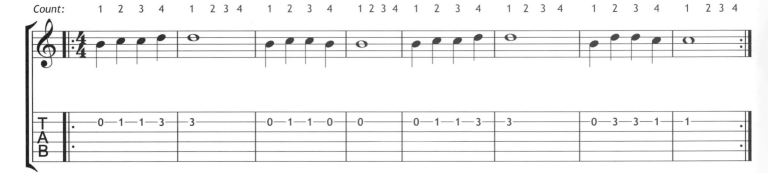

ALTERNATING 1ST AND 2ND STRINGS

The next two tunes will help you get used to moving between the two strings, practise them slowly and accurately.

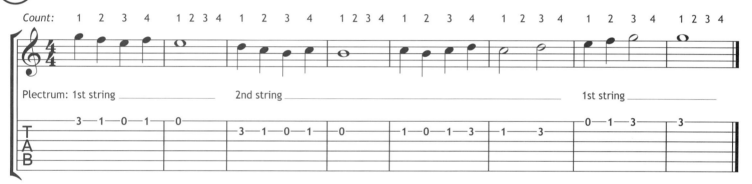

Ties

A curved line joining notes of the same pitch together is called a tie. Two notes joined in this way will sound like one longer note (do not strike the string again for the second note). So a two-beat note tied to a one-beat note will sound like one continuous three-beat note.

Ties are often used to extend the sound of a note across a barline.

The music shown below offers a few examples of the way ties may be used. The timing is quite tricky so follow the music while you listen to the CD demonstration.

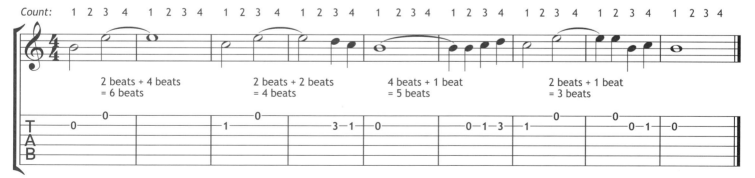

21

C TO G AND D TO F STRETCHING EXERCISE

This stretching exercise will help you prepare for the next piece – 'Retro Surf Band'.

Leave each note sounding for as long as possible to create a 'smooth' joined-up effect between the notes. Playing a piece of music so that it sounds 'smooth and seamless' is called playing **Legato**, from the Italian word meaning linked or joined.

In Bar 2, you will need to practise keeping the 'pad' of your third finger out of the way of the 1st string so that the note 'F' sounds clearly. (This will become very important in producing clear sounding chords later in the book.) The exercise is demonstrated on the CD.

Track 30

Retro Surf Band

In 'Retro Surf Band' look out for the C to G stretch in bar 1 and again towards the end of the piece, also the D to F stretch in bar 6. There are ties used in bars 11 and 19.

Checking a new song for repeat signs is a good habit to develop.

Follow the music while you listen to the CD. There are three CD versions of this piece, the last one is quite fast so 'have a go' and don't worry if you can't keep up, you can always come back to it later.

The symbol ⌒ shown over the last note of the piece is called a fermata or pause. It means hold the note as long as you wish or until it fades out naturally.

Track 31-32 *Retro Surf Band*

*Try the **2nd String** section of the Quiz on page 107.*

3RD STRING – NOTES G AND A

Track 33

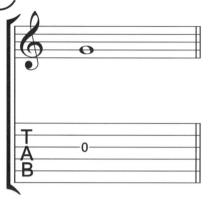

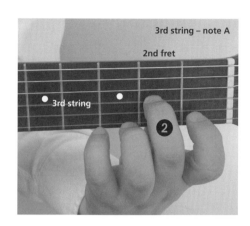

Note G
Open
3rd string

Note A
Second finger, 2nd fret
3rd string

Track 34

The open 3rd string is the note '**G**', it is separated from the '**G**' on the **1st string (3rd fret)** by an interval known as an octave.* The notes share the same 'letter-name' – they sound similar when played but the 1st string '**G**' has a higher pitch – listen to the CD demonstration to hear what is meant.

With these extra notes under your belt, see if you can master the following three exercises.

Track 35 – *3rd String Exercise*

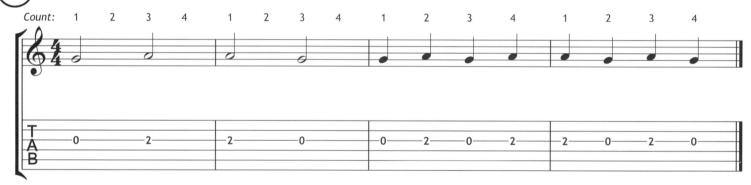

Track 36 – *2nd and 3rd Strings Exercise*

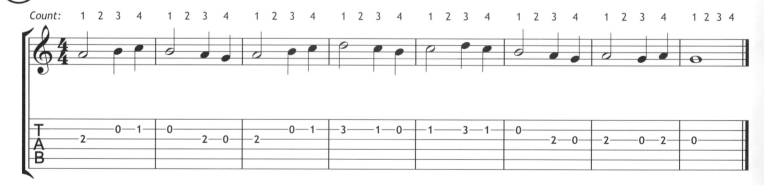

24

* They are eight notes apart (inclusive) i.e. **G**, A, B, C, D, E, F, **G**; hence the word octave from the Latin word Octo (meaning eight).

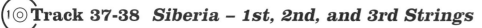

Track 37-38 *Siberia – 1st, 2nd, and 3rd Strings*

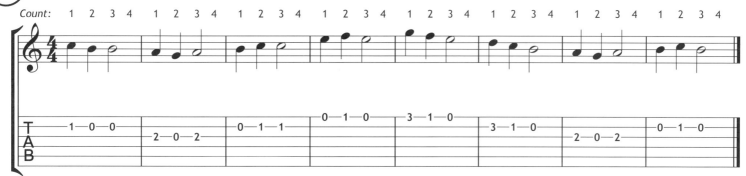

Repeat symbols

The symbol ⅍ in the second bar of 'The Cave' means repeat the preceding bar.

It is called a **measure-repeat sign** (or bar-repeat sign).

In this next piece there are five bars of music but you have only two different bars to learn. You can keep your left-hand third finger pressed down throughout the piece.

Track 39-40 *The Cave*

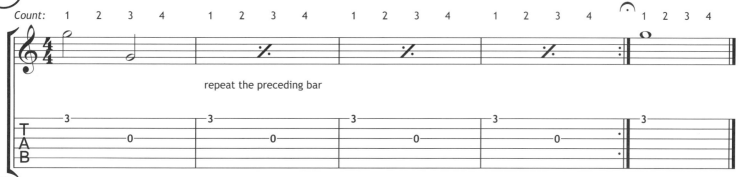

repeat the preceding bar

Track 41-42 *Big Ben*

Track 43-44 *'Scalish' Melody*

NEW TIME SIGNATURE $\frac{3}{4}$

All the pieces in the book so far have been in $\frac{4}{4}$ time.

The next pieces have a time signature of $\frac{3}{4}$ also known as Waltz time.

Track 45-46

There are three quarter-note (crotchet) beats per bar. Remember that a dotted half-note has a time value of three beats (see page 18).

Follow the music while you listen to the CD demonstration.

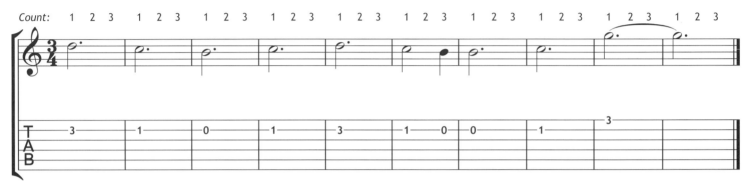

Track 47

New note 'A' on the 1st string

Notes that are too high (or too low) to be placed within the stave are written on (or between) short lines called **Ledger Lines**.

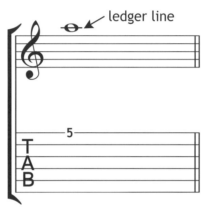

ledger line

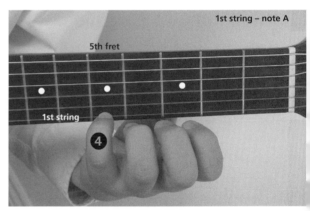

1st string – note A
5th fret
1st string

Second position

When you use your left-hand fourth finger to play the new note 'A', your hand is in 'second position'.

In **'first position'** your **first finger** is over the **1st fret**, your **second finger** over the **2nd fret** and so on. All the fingering in the book, so far, has been in first position.

In **'second position'** your **first finger** is over the **2nd fret**, your **second finger** over the **3rd fret**, your **third finger** over the **4th fret** and your **fourth finger** over the **5th fret**.

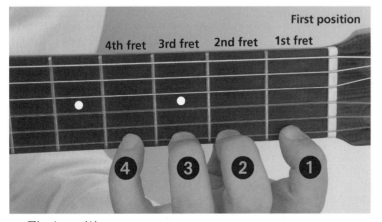

First position

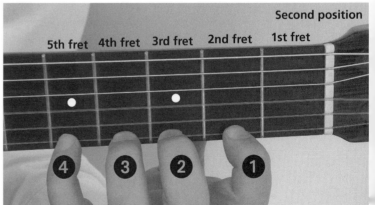

Second position

Track 48-49: *Liebestraum* (composed by Franz Liszt (1811 – 1886))

Bars 19 and 20 are played in second-position.

In bar 19, use your left-hand fourth finger for the note 'A' (on the 1st string 5th fret).

In bar 20 you will need to stretch with your first finger to reach the lower 'A' (on the 3rd string 2nd fret). At the start of bar 21, change to your second finger to hold-down the same note 'A', so that your left-hand is now in first position for the rest of the piece.

A **Rest** denotes a period of silence, where the musician plays nothing.

In the same way played notes have a time-value – so do rests.

Below are some of the more common rests explained.

Note Values:			Corresponding Rests:	
o	a **whole-note**	(or semibreve)	▬	lasts **four beats**
𝅗𝅥	a **half-note**	(or minim)	▬	lasts **two beats**
♩	a **quarter-note**	(or crotchet)	𝄽	lasts **one beat**
♪	an **eighth-note**	(or quaver)	𝄾	lasts a **half beat**
𝅘𝅥𝅯	a **sixteenth-note**	(or semiquaver)	𝄿	lasts a **quarter of a beat**

Left-hand Finger Muting

Where a rest is shown you must stop the strings from sounding. One technique to achieve this is known as 'Left-hand Finger Muting'.

For example, in bar 1 of the Rest Exercise below, play the open-string 'E'. Then, on the first beat of bar 2, stop the sound of the string by placing the pads of your fingers flat across the strings as shown in the photo (right).

You may find this technique challenging at first, but with practice you should master it.

This is demonstrated on the CD.

Left-hand Finger Muting Technique

Track 50

The mute only needs to be in place for a moment so you can remove it almost immediately in readiness to play the next note. Practise it as one quick 'one-off' moment.

Track 51 *Rest Exercise*

Now try the 3rd String section of the Quiz on page 108.

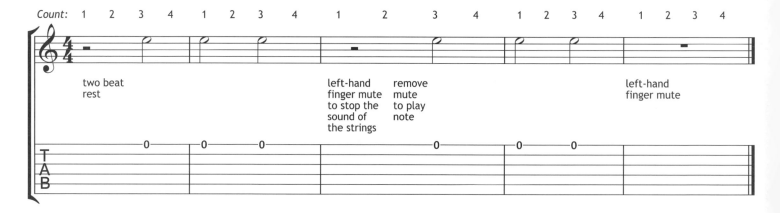

Track 52-54 *It's You*

The rest symbol at the start of bar 1 lasts for two beats, so **you** start playing on the 3rd beat of the bar. Listen to the CD demonstration to hear what is meant. Bars 3, 5 and 7 have similar timings.

When you reach the end of bar 16, leave your third finger on the 1st string, 3rd fret while you place your first finger on the 2nd string, 1st fret to play bar 17.

From bar 17 to the end, strum both the 1st and 2nd strings simultaneously with your plectrum while you place your left-hand fingers as directed in the tab.

For this section leave your left-hand third finger on the 1st string at the 3rd fret – this will act as a pivot for your first finger.

4TH STRING – NOTES D, E AND F

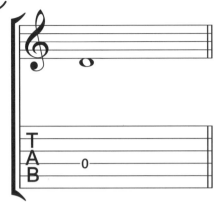

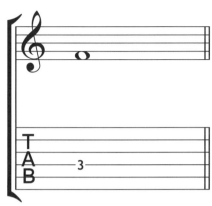

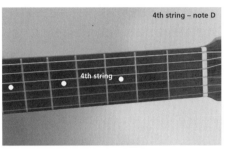

Note D
Open
4th string

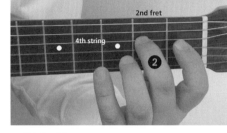

Note E
Second finger, 2nd fret
4th string

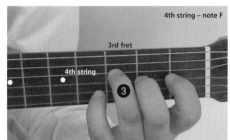

Note F
Third finger, 3rd fret
4th string

The three notes 'D', 'E' and 'F' shown above, are an octave lower than the 'D', 'E' and 'F' you learnt earlier in the book. Work through the following exercises until you are comfortable moving between all four strings.

Track 56 *Exercise 1 – 4th String*

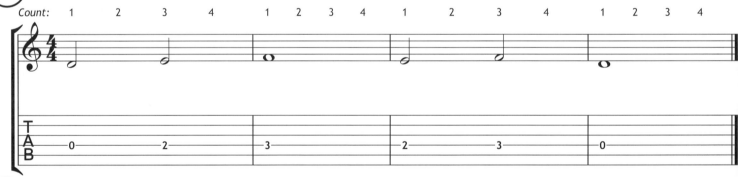

Track 57 *Exercise 2 – 4th String*

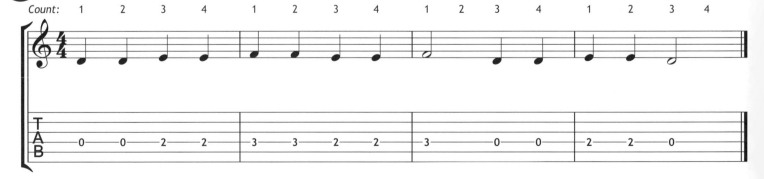

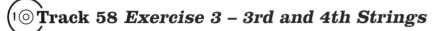

Track 58 *Exercise 3 – 3rd and 4th Strings*

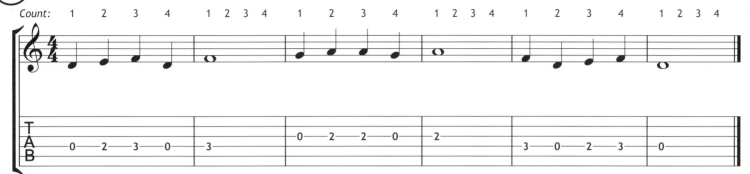

Track 59 *Exercise 4 – 2nd, 3rd and 4th Strings*

Track 60 *Exercise 5 – 1st, 2nd, 3rd and 4th Strings*

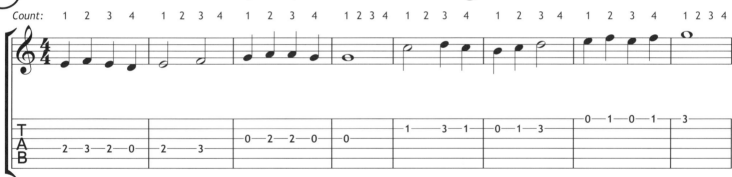

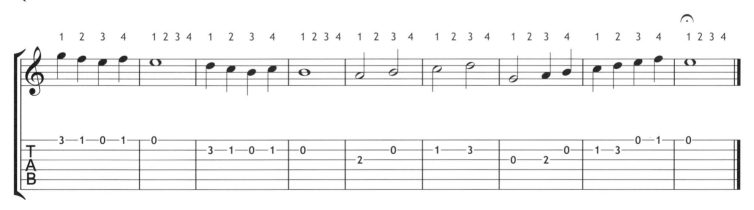

ACCIDENTALS – SHARP SYMBOLS*

A sharp symbol ♯ placed to the left of a note on the music stave raises its pitch by a semitone (one fret). Notice that F♯ is one fret higher up the neck (towards you) than F. The effect of a sharp symbol starts from where it first appears in the bar and lasts until it is cancelled by the next barline.

There are two new notes to learn for the next song: F♯ on the 1st string and G♯ on the 3rd string.

 **Track 61**

Note F

 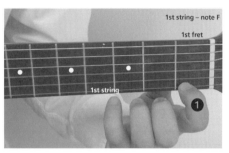

New Note F♯

 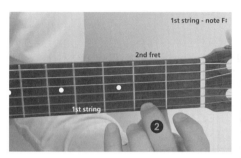

New note G♯

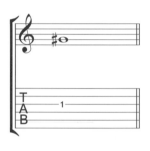 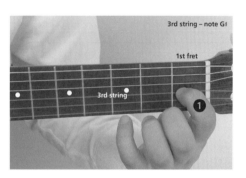

First-and Second-Time Repeat Bars

First and second time bars are a handy way to write a section of music that repeats but has a slightly altered ending on the second time around.

For the first time through, play the first-time bar.

For the second time through, play the second-time bar (omitting the first-time bar).

For example, the bars **1**, **2**, **3**, **4**, and **5** shown below:

			1.	2.
1	2	3	4	5

Using the first and second time repeat bars they would be played in the following order:

1	2	3	4	1	2	3	5

* Sharps belong to a class of musical symbols called accidentals (you can read more about these on pages 61-62).

Track 62-63 *Through Chopin's Eyes*

Take note of the first and second time repeats (bars 16 and 17).

On the first time through, play the first-time bar and then play from the start again. On the second time through, play the second-time bar (omitting the first-time bar).

In bar 7 remember that a dot placed to the right of a note extends its time-value by a half.

Listen to the backing track while you follow the music to make sure you have understood the way the repeat structure works.

play this bar on the 2nd time through

play from bar 18 again

left-hand finger mute

strum both the 1st and 2nd strings simultaneously

EIGHTH-NOTES

An **Eighth-note** (or **Quaver**) lasts for **half a beat**.

It has a single 'flag' attached to its stem

Groups of eighth-notes may be joined together with **beams** for ease of reading.

All the plectrum strokes in the book so far have been **down-strokes (⊓)**. Remember that down-strokes start on the upper side of the string to be played, and then proceed downwards (towards the floor).

Up-strokes (∨) start on the lower side of the string to be played, and then proceed upwards (away from the floor).

You will need to use a combination of up- and down-strokes to achieve any speed or dexterity with your plectrum technique.

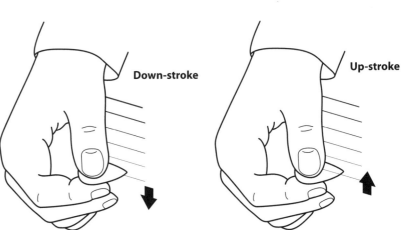

When to use an up-stroke.

Tap your foot to a $\frac{4}{4}$ beat (1, 2, 3, 4) while you count out loud 1 & 2 & 3 & 4 &

The numbers **1, 2, 3, 4** may be thought of as **down-beats** and the **&**s as **up-beats**.

Play a down-stroke on a down-beat.

Play an up-stroke on an up-beat.

Imagine your plectrum hand attached to your foot by a string. **When your foot goes down use a down-stroke, when your foot goes up use an up-stroke.** †

† Your accuracy at striking the correct string will improve with practice. It is worth persevering even if some of the plectrum strokes seem to be less even than others to begin with.

Track 64 *Eighth-notes on the 1st and 2nd strings.*

Track 65 *Eighth-notes on the 1st, 2nd and 3rd strings.*

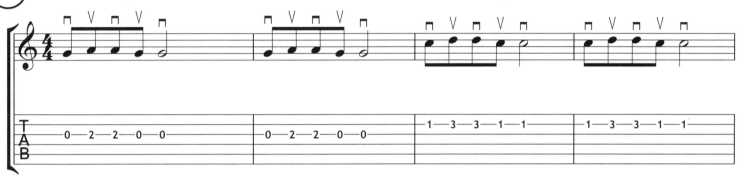

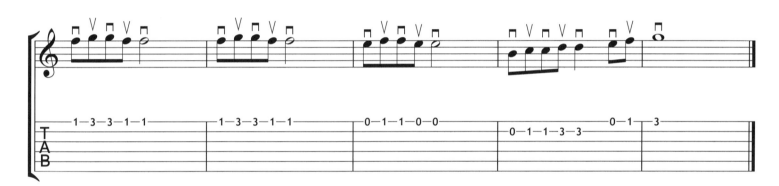

Track 66 *Eighth-notes on the 1st, 2nd, 3rd and 4th strings.*

CHANGING TO A HIGHER STRING ON A 'PLECTRUM UP-STROKE'

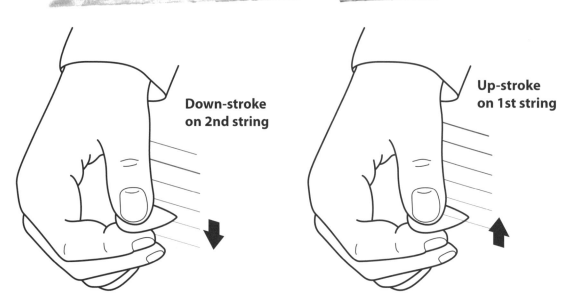

Down-stroke on 2nd string

Up-stroke on 1st string

Playing these exercises will be a challenge for your plectrum technique, so start practising at a slow tempo.

The note 'B' occurs on a down-beat, play it with a down-stroke, the note 'E' occurs on an up-beat, play it with an up-stroke.

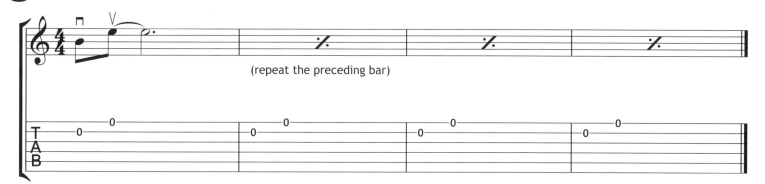

(repeat the preceding bar)

The next exercise requires you to change from the 2nd
string on a down-stroke to the 1st string on an up-stroke,
and then back again to the second string on a
down–stroke.

Start by practising at a slow tempo.

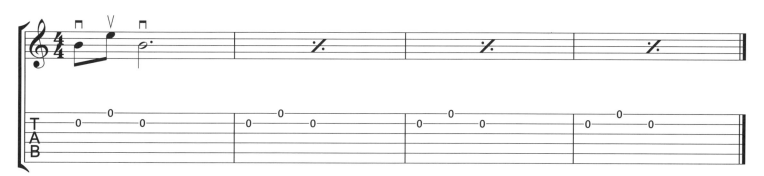

You will need to have mastered these quick plectrum
changes between the 4th, 3rd and 2nd strings in order
to play bars 21–24 of the song on the next page.

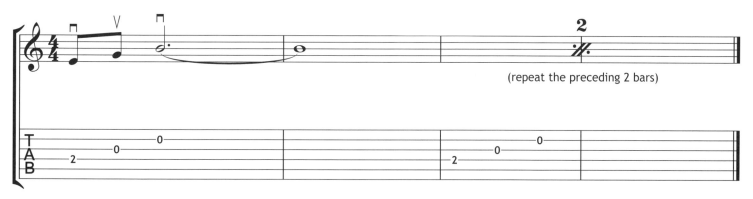

(repeat the preceding 2 bars)

Track 68-70 *A Silent Mind*

The symbol $\overset{4}{\cancel{////.}}$ in the middle of bars 29-32 means repeat the preceding four bars.

Look out for the second set of repeat symbols ‖: :‖ between bars 13 and 36.

Check that you have understood the way the repeats work by following the music while you listen to the song on the CD.

In this exercise, your left-hand fingers stay in the same position for two bars at a time.

For example: keep your left-hand fingers in the same position for bars **1 and 2**, change for bars **3 and 4**, play 'open strings' for bars **5 and 6** and so on...

In bars 2, 4, 6 and 8 strum the 1st and 2nd strings simultaneously.

The notes used in this exercise will help you prepare for the left-hand finger positions you will use to form chords later in the book. For example bars 1 and 2 form part of a chord called 'D Major', make sure the pad of your third finger is clear of the 1st string so that it sounds clearly.*

◉Track 71

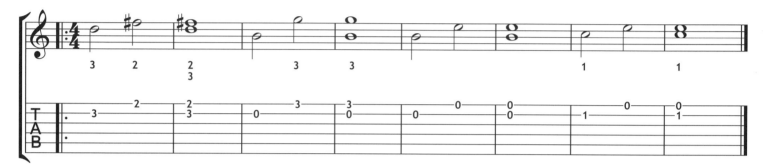

*Now try the **4th String** section of the Quiz on page 110.*

Left-Hand Pressure Mute

In the last bar of 'Not That Vain', stop the sound on beat 3 of the bar by relaxing the pressure of your second and third fingers against the fretboard until the sound stops.

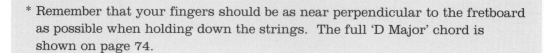

* Remember that your fingers should be as near perpendicular to the fretboard as possible when holding down the strings. The full 'D Major' chord is shown on page 74.

Track 72-73 *Not That Vain*

From bar 9 to the end of this next piece, strike both the 1st and 2nd strings simultaneously with your plectrum. Use down-strums throughout.

The left-hand finger movements from bar 9 may be tricky to start with so practise them slowly until they become familiar. Check the tuning of your guitar again, before playing along with the CD.

Relax the pressure of your second and third fingers against the fretboard to mute the strings.

CHORDS

Chords are groups of two or more notes played together.*

The chords in this exercise only use the 1st, 2nd, 3rd and 4th strings so be careful not to catch the 5th or 6th string.

Start each chord with a down-strum (near the bridge) from the 4th string and end with the 1st string.

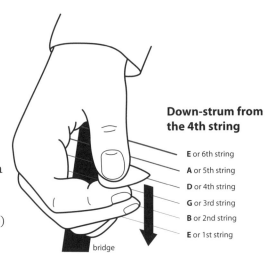

Down-strum from the 4th string

E or 6th string
A or 5th string
D or 4th string
G or 3rd string
B or 2nd string
E or 1st string

bridge

Find the finger positions for the chords from the Tab. Notice that only the 1st string changes in each chord; the 2nd, 3rd and 4th strings are all played 'open' throughout.

The photos below serve as a quick reference to make sure you have everything in the right place.
Make sure your guitar is in tune.

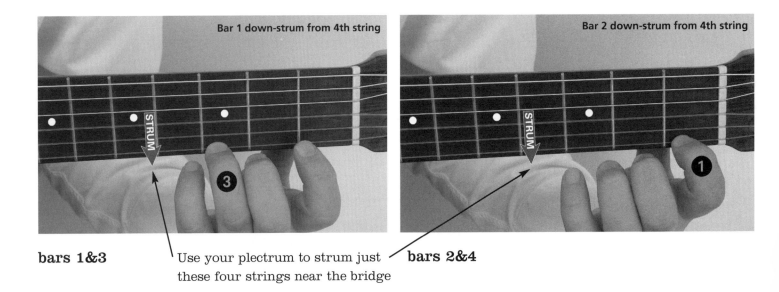

Bar 1 down-strum from 4th string   Bar 2 down-strum from 4th string

bars 1&3   Use your plectrum to strum just   bars 2&4
these four strings near the bridge

Track 74

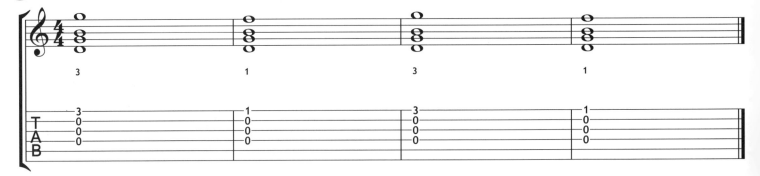

* Diad is the term for two notes played simultaneously. Triad is the term for three notes played simultaneously.

CHORD BOXES

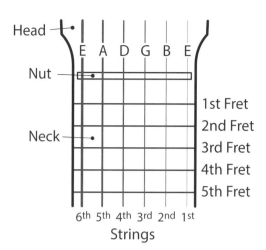

Chord boxes are diagrams of the **guitar neck viewed head upwards** and **facing you** (as illustrated).

The two horizontal lines at the top of the box represent the nut.

The single horizontal lines represent the fret-wires and the vertical lines represent the strings.

The fingers of your left hand are numbered 1, 2, 3 and 4 (see diagram).

The numbered circles represent finger positions on the fretboard.

Strings marked with an 'O' should be played open.

Strings marked with an 'X' should not be played.

Chord boxes are used in many books of popular music repertoire. The two chords you played on page 42 are shown here in chord box form.

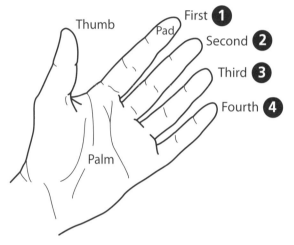

Easy G

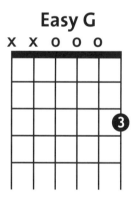

X X O O O

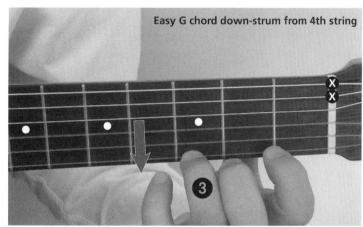

Easy G chord down-strum from 4th string

Easy G⁷

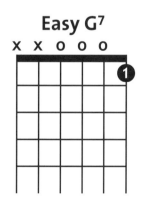

X X O O O

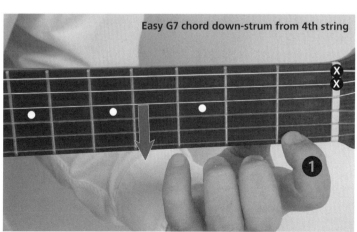

Easy G7 chord down-strum from 4th string

STRUMMING/ RHYTHM SLASHES

A chord may be represented above the music stave by a '**chord symbol**' which is often an abbreviation, for example: **G Major** is abbreviated to **G** and **G Seventh** to **G7** etc...*

Rhythm slash notation represents a 'shorthand' way of suggesting the rhythm to be strummed. The stave has only one line because it doesn't need to show individual notes.

The chord symbols tell you which chord to play and the chord-boxes tell you which notes comprise those chords.

The rhythm slash 'note heads' are a stylised version of those used in traditional music notation. They are shown below (this is a demonstration, don't try to play it).

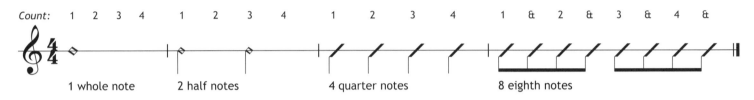

The chord exercise you played on page 42 is shown here in rhythm-slash notation with chord symbols. The benefit of this notation is its simplicity.

First, memorise the finger positions for Easy G and G7 from the chord boxes.

Then read the chord symbols from above the stave, and strum the chords as indicated by the rhythm-slashes. This is demonstrated on the CD.

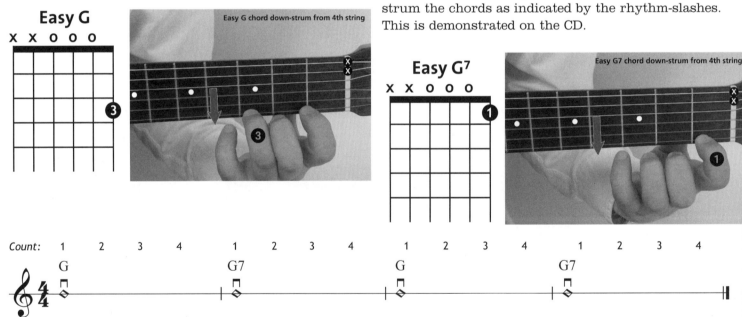

* Full versions of these chords are shown on pages 78-79.

EASY C CHORD

Learn the finger positions for the 'Easy C' chord from the chord box, and then practise forming the 'chord shape'.*

Check the sound of your 'Easy C' chord against the CD demonstration. Practise changing back and forth between the 'Easy C' and 'Easy G7' chords before playing along with the CD backing track.

The chord box for 'Easy C' shows that the 1st and 3rd strings are open, so make sure they can vibrate freely without your fingers hampering them – by keeping your fingers perpendicular to the fretboard you are more likely to be successful.

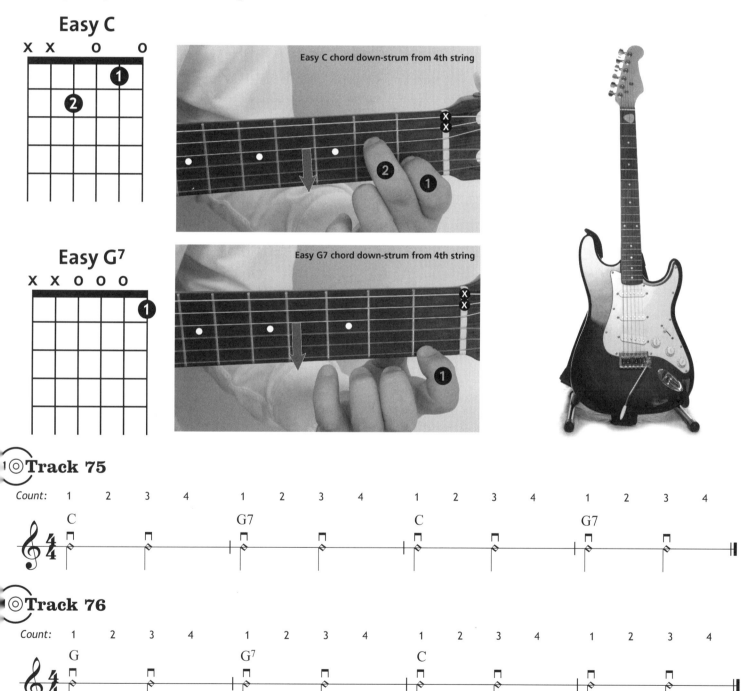

Easy C

Easy C chord down-strum from 4th string

Easy G⁷

Easy G7 chord down-strum from 4th string

◎ Track 75

Count: 1 2 3 4 | 1 2 3 4 | 1 2 3 4 | 1 2 3 4

C   G7   C   G7

◎ Track 76

Count: 1 2 3 4 | 1 2 3 4 | 1 2 3 4 | 1 2 3 4

G   G⁷   C

> * The term 'chord shape' is a shorthand way of referring to the shape made by your fingers when they form a chord. The full version of the C chord is shown on page 54.

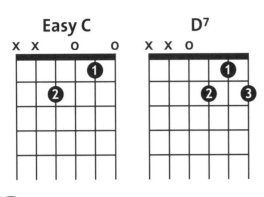

Easy C   D⁷

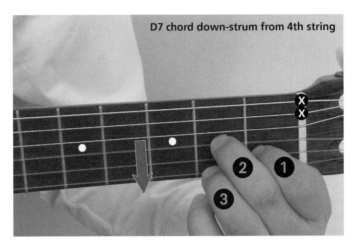

D7 chord down-strum from 4th string

⊙ **Track 77**

Easy C to **D7** change.

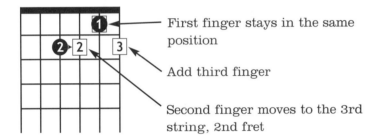

First finger stays in the same position

Add third finger

Second finger moves to the 3rd string, 2nd fret

Changing between 'C' and 'D7' will be easier if you notice that your **first finger** remains on the **2nd string, 1st fret**.

Practise changing smoothly between 'C' and 'D7' by using your **first finger as a pivot** and moving just your **second and third fingers** (see diagram).

The key to the diagram is as follows:

The white numbers in black circles i.e. ❶ represent the finger positions of the first chord (in this case the Easy C chord).

The black numbers in white squares i.e. ☐1 represent the finger positions of the second chord.

Fingers common to both chords are indicated by the graphic ❶ (in other words, a white number, in a black circle, surrounded by a box).

Arrows show the direction in which your fingers should move.

Now try the C to D7 exercise.

⊙ **Track 78**

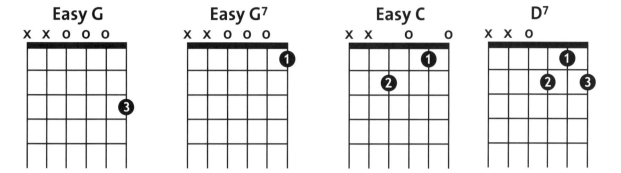

In the following song, the rhythm slashes and chord symbols are shown above the stave. The music and lyrics are shown for guidance only, so just play the chords.

Use down-strums throughout.*

Track 79-80 *Waiting For The Rains*

*Try the **Chords** section of the Quiz on page 112.*

> * Many books of popular music are offered in a similar format to that shown above (melody-line, chords and lyrics). However, they rarely offer a strumming-pattern so you have to choose your own. As a rule: if it sounds right, then it is right.

The guitar parts for 'Arpeggio Groove' and 'Blues Style' sound best when the strings are allowed to ring on until the next chord change (i.e. let all the notes from bars 1 and 2 keep sounding until you start to play bar 3). Listen to the CD demonstration to hear what is meant. When the notes of a chord are broken up and played in this 'staggered' way, they are called **arpeggios**.

Track 81-82 *Arpeggio Groove*

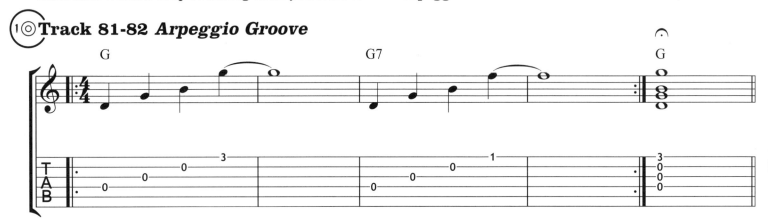

Track 83-84 *Blues Style*

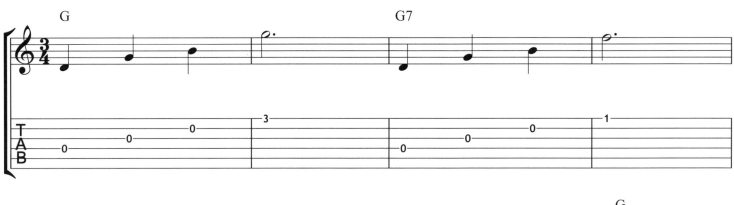

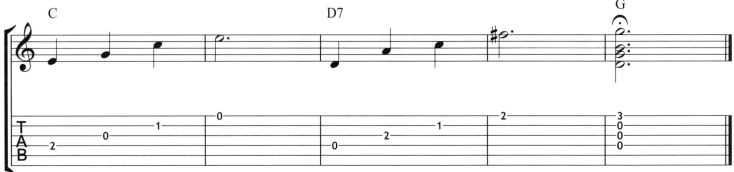

Remember that the time signature $\frac{3}{4}$ indicates three beats per bar.

D⁷

x x o

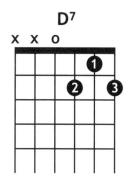

D7 chord down-strum from 4th string

Easy G⁷

x x o o o

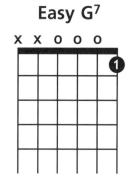

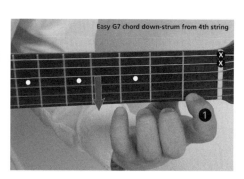

Easy G7 chord down-strum from 4th string

Playing this piece will provide you with an opportunity to practise changing between D7 and Easy G7. Check that your guitar is in tune with the CD before playing-along.

Track 85-86

Track 87 Right-Hand Palm Mute

In the next exercise, the first beat of Bar 1 is played with the 1st string 'fretted'* (at the 3rd fret) and the 2nd string open. In cases where you are playing a combination of 'open' and 'fretted' strings it is convenient to use a right-hand palm mute (see diagram, right) to stop the sound.

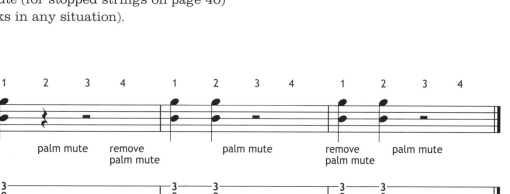

For example, in bar 1 play the notes B and G simultaneously on beat 1. Then on beat 2 place your right-hand on the strings with just enough pressure to stop the sound. Aim your plectrum so that it comes to rest in the correct position to play the next notes – in this case resting on the 2nd string (to play bar 2).

You have now learned three types of mute:
- The left-hand mute (for open strings on page 28).
- The left-hand finger-pressure mute (for stopped strings on page 40)
- The right-hand palm mute (works in any situation).

Track 88

Count: 1 2 3 4 | 1 2 3 4 | 1 2 3 4 | 1 2 3 4

palm mute to stop sound | remove palm mute | palm mute | remove palm mute | palm mute | remove palm mute | palm mute

* When a string is held down at a fret, it is said to be 'fretted'.

5TH STRING – NOTES A, B AND C

The note 'A' on the 1st string was too high to be placed in the stave and was therefore written on a ledger line above it.

These three notes are too low to be placed on the stave and are written on ledger lines below it.

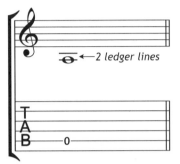
← 2 ledger lines

← 1 ledger line

← 1 ledger line

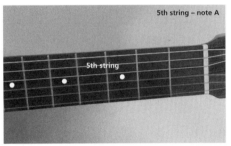

5th string – note A

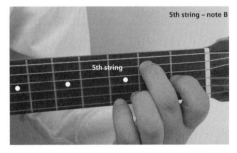

5th string – note B

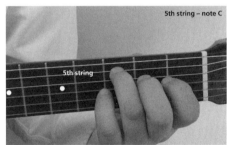

5th string – note C

Note A
Open
5th string

Note B
Second finger, 2nd fret
5th string

Note C
Third finger, 3rd fret
5th string

🔟 Track 90 *5th String Exercise 1*

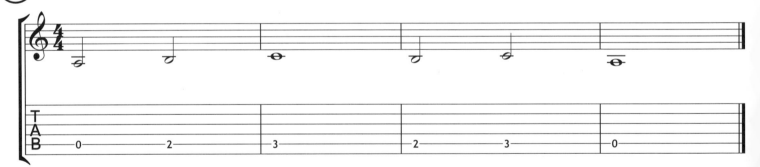

🔟 Track 91 *5th String Exercise 2*

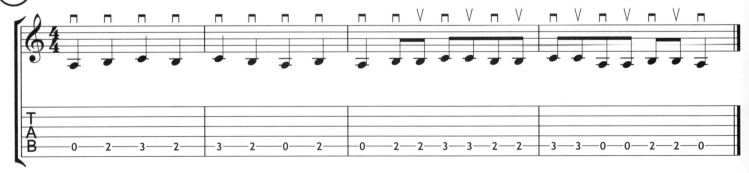

⦿ Track 92 *Exercise on Five Strings*

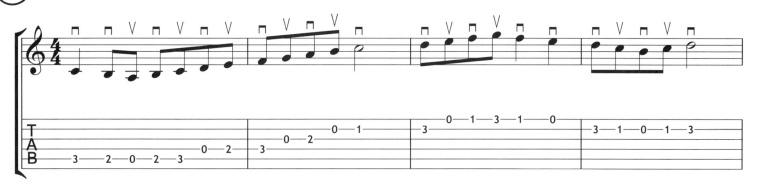

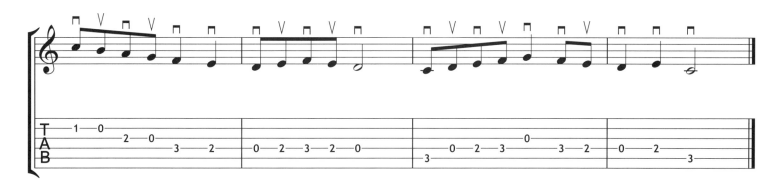

NEW NOTE C# ON THE 5TH STRING

⦿ Track 93

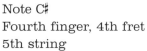

5th string – note C#

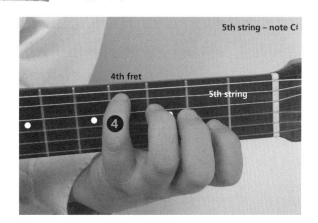

4th fret

5th string

Note C#
Fourth finger, 4th fret
5th string

⦿ Track 94-95 *Fourth Finger Exercise*

Play four times through.

| Count: | 1 | & | 2 | 3 | & | 4 | 1 | & | 2 | 3 | 4 |

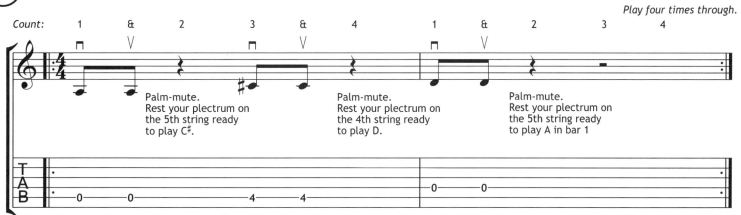

Palm-mute.
Rest your plectrum on
the 5th string ready
to play C#.

Palm-mute.
Rest your plectrum on
the 4th string ready
to play D.

Palm-mute.
Rest your plectrum on
the 5th string ready
to play A in bar 1

C MAJOR 7 AND F MAJOR 7 CHORDS

Track 1

C Maj⁷

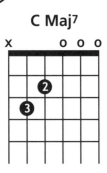

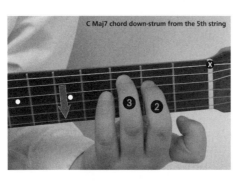

C Maj7 chord down-strum from the 5th string

F Maj⁷

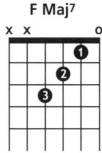

F Maj7 chord down-strum from 4th string

The chord of C Major7 may be abbreviated to the chord-symbol C Maj7 and F Major7 to F Maj7. Find the finger-positions for both chords from the chord boxes above. Remember that open strings marked with an 'X' should not be played. Changing between C Maj7 and F Maj7 will be easier if you notice the similar 'shape' formed by your second and third fingers for both chords. They change strings but stay on the 2nd and 3rd frets respectively (see diagram).

C Maj7 to **F Maj7** change.

Add first finger for FMaj7

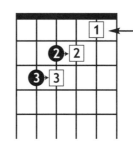

Track 2

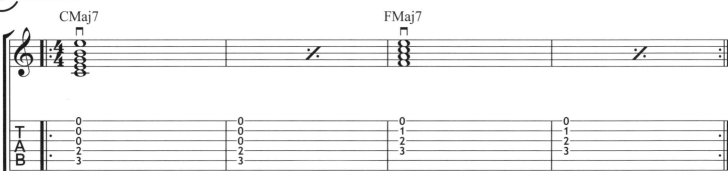

The technique used in 'Flying' creates the effect of hearing a simple 'bass line'.

Form the chord C Maj7 at the beginning of bar 1.

On the first beat play the note 'C' on the 5th string. Let your plectrum come to rest on the 4th string in readiness to play the rest of the chord on the second beat.

For bar 3, play the whole chord with one strum (as indicated). It is easier to play this than to explain it, so follow the music while you listen to the CD demonstration.

Track 3-4 _Flying_

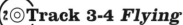

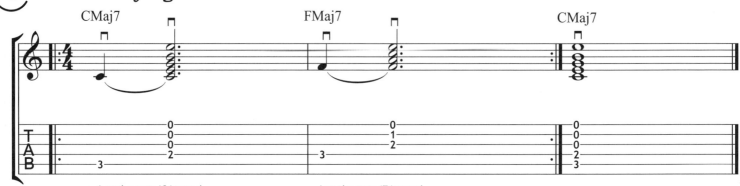

Let the note 'C' sound for the whole bar.

Let the note 'F' sound for the whole bar.

② ◎ Track 5-6 *Papillon (chord part)*

Remember that the time-signature $\frac{3}{4}$ indicates three beats per bar. The chord part for 'Papillon' is played in a similar way to the piece 'Flying'.

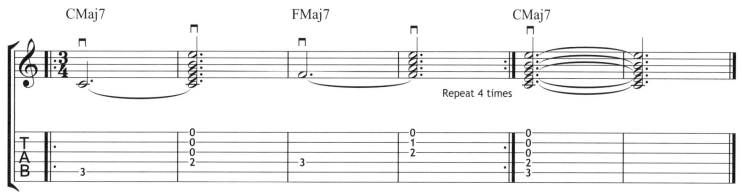

Allow the note C to 'sound'
throughout bars 1 and 2.

② ◎ Track 7-8 *Papillon (melody part)*

To play the melody part, you will have to train your plectrum hand to swap strings quickly (especially in bars 4 and 10). Expect to spend a little time getting this right.

C MAJOR AND A MINOR CHORDS

Track 9

C

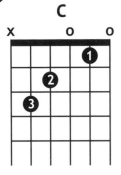

C chord (full version) down-strum from 5th string

Am

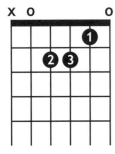

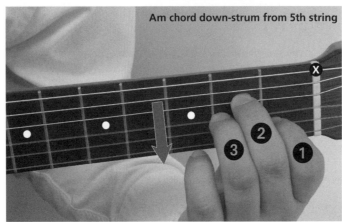

Am chord down-strum from 5th string

The C Major chord may be abbreviated to the chord symbol 'C' and A minor to 'Am'.*
It is said that minor chords tend to have a sad sound.

Find the finger positions for these chords from the chord boxes.

You may recognise the shape formed by your first and second fingers in the 'C' chord box from the 'easy C chord'.

To change between the chords 'C' and 'Am' you move only your third finger; the first and second fingers stay in the same position for both chords (see diagram).

C to Am change.

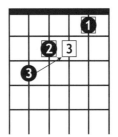

First and second fingers stay in same position.

Track 10 *Exercise 1*

	C		Am		C		Am	

* Arrangers tend to use a lowercase 'm' when describing minor chords and a capital M when describing Major chords.

D MINOR CHORD

The D minor chord may be abbreviated to the chord symbol Dm.

Find the finger positions for Dm from the chord box.

You need only move your first and third fingers to change between F Maj7 and Dm; your second finger stays in the same place (the 3rd string 2nd fret) for both chords.

Dm

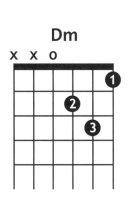

Dm chord down-strum from 4th string

F Maj7

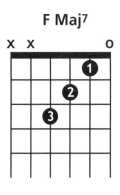

F Maj7 chord down-strum from 4th string

 **to Dm change.**

Second finger stays in same position

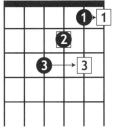

Track 12 *Exercise 2*

Practise changing between C, Am, F Maj7 and Dm with this exercise.

Track 13 *Exercise 3*

Track 14

Learn the finger positions for Asus2 from the chord box.

When changing from C to Asus2 (i.e.: bars 10 to 11), notice that your second finger stays in the same position for both chords.

C

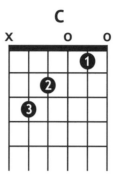

A sus²

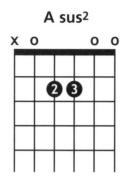

Track 15-16 *Change Your Fate*

This song uses many of the chords you have learned so far. The chord boxes are shown here as a reminder. At bar 10 look out for the new strumming pattern.

Change from playing one strum per bar to four strums per bar.

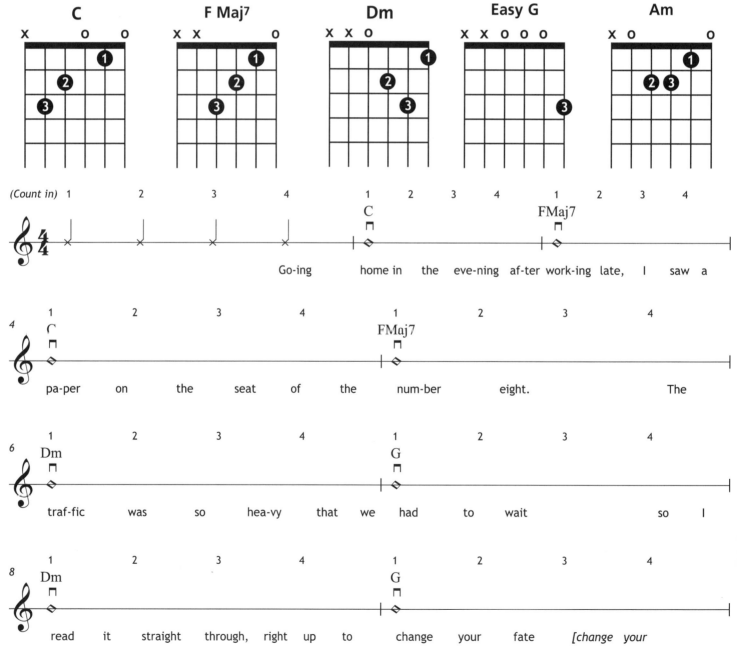

56

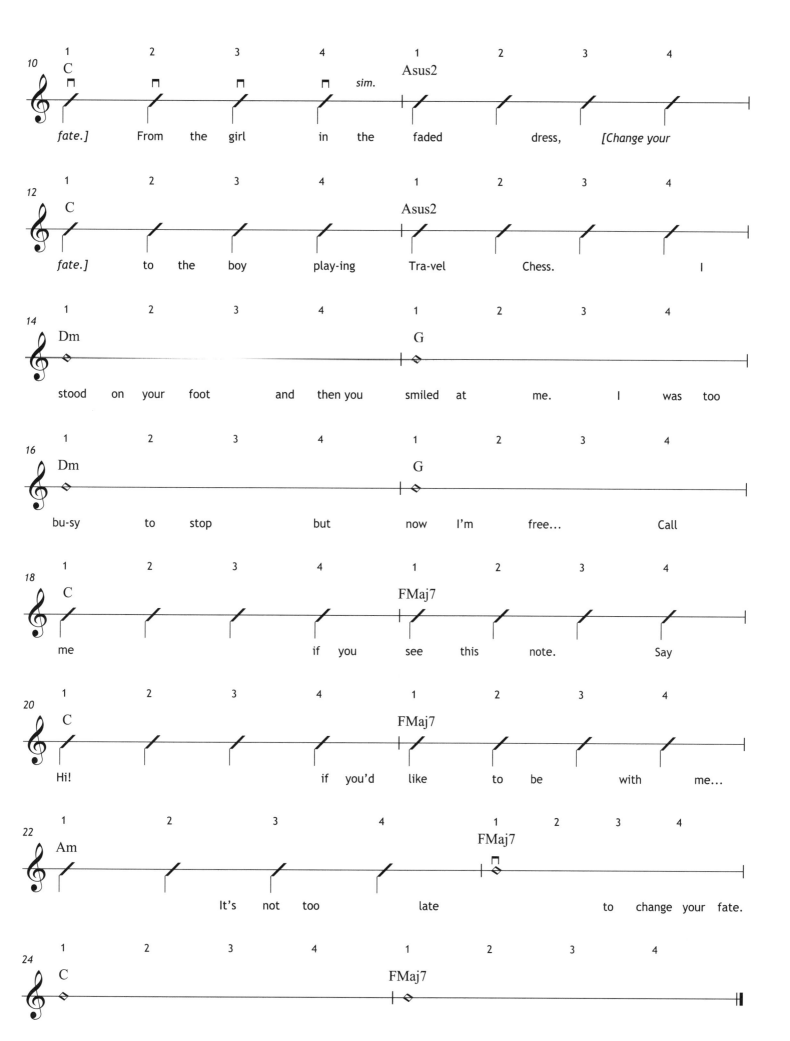

D MINOR 6 CHORD

Dm⁶

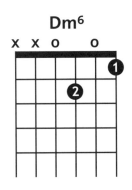

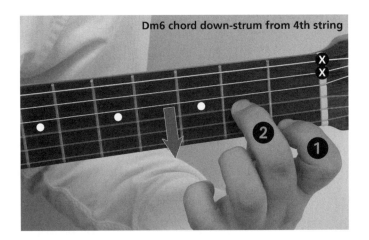

Dm6 chord down-strum from 4th string

The D minor 6 chord may be abbreviated to Dm6. The first and second finger positions for Dm6 are the same as for Dm.

Find the finger positions for Dm6 from the chord box.

Keep the pad of your second finger out of the way of the 2nd string – allowing it to sound clearly.

Counting Exercise

The timing of this exercise is demonstrated on the CD; it will be easier to learn if you remember that the first beat of bar 1 is a quarter-note (crotchet) rest (i.e. a count of one beat before you play) The same is true of bar 3.

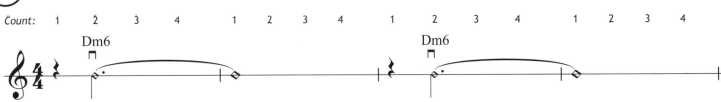

Count: 1 2 3 4   1 2 3 4   1 2 3 4   1 2 3 4

Dm6   Dm6

The timing of this song is similar to the last exercise and is demonstrated on the CD.

Changing between the chords Am and Dm6 will be easier if you notice that your first and second fingers remain in the same shape but on different strings for both chords.

The chord part is repetitive so that you can concentrate on counting the beats.

Check that your guitar is in tune and then play-along with the practice track.

There are three versions of this piece, the last one has a rap vocal line. The ability to concentrate on your part while playing-along with a vocal line will be useful for those who want to play in a band.

Track 19

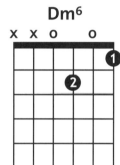

Am to **Dm6** change.

Move your first and second fingers together (in the same shape).

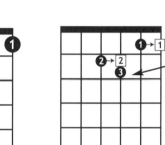

Remove your third finger for Dm6.

Track 20-21 *Ich, Ni, San, Chi (Bling!)*

Practice version – play twice.
Main version – play twice.
Vocal version – play 4 times.

*Now try the 5th **String** section of the Quiz on page 114.*

6TH STRING — NOTES E, F AND G

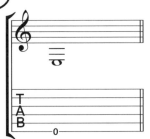

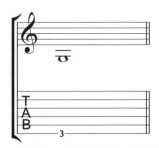

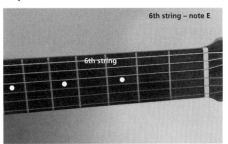

Note E
Open
1st string

Note F
First finger, 1st fret
1st string

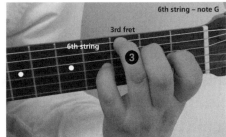

Note G
Third finger, 3rd fret
1st string

Track 23 *6th String Exercise 1*

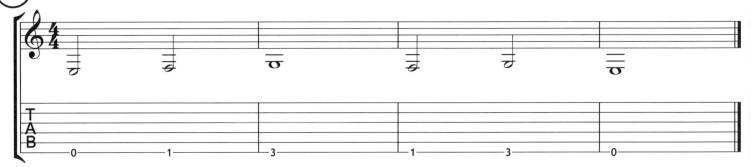

Track 24 *6th String Exercise 2*

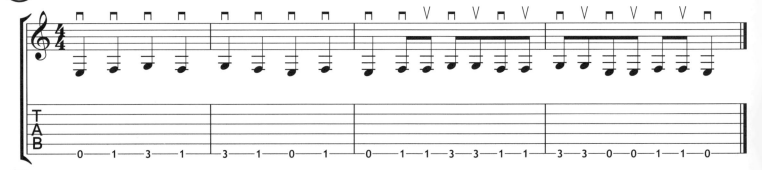

Track 25 *5th and 6th String Exercise 3*

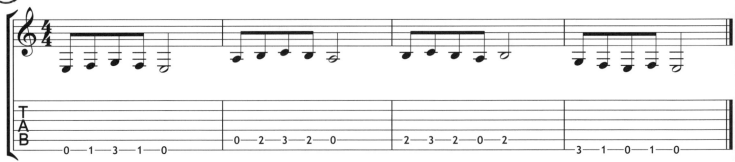

Track 26

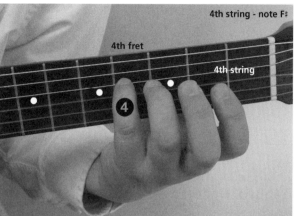

New Note F♯
Fourth finger, 4th fret
4th string

Track 27 _Key Signatures_

In the following exercise all the F's are sharpened. This is the scale of G Major.

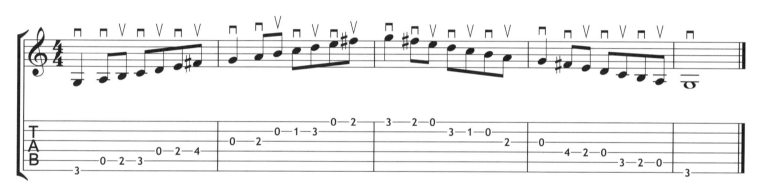

When it is known that all the Fs will be 'sharpened' in a piece of music, it makes sense to tell the musician at the beginning. This is done with a **key signature**.*

G Major has a key signature of one sharp – F♯ – which is written on the top line at the start of each stave;

this means that all Fs (in all registers**) are raised to F♯.

Here is the scale of G Major again, but this time shown with the key signature of G Major at the beginning.

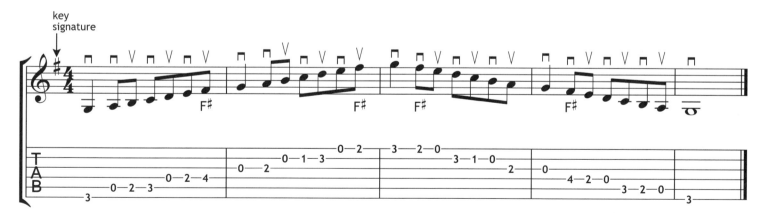

* There's more about scales on page 100
** In this particular context 'in all registers' means all 'F' notes whether on the 1st string, the 4th string etc.

ACCIDENTALS – FLAT SYMBOLS ♭

The 'flat' symbol ♭ seen to the left of a note on the stave lowers its pitch by a semitone (one fret). B♭ is pronounced 'B flat'.

Like the sharp symbol it is called an accidental and is subject to the same rules. The effect of a flat sign starts from where it appears in the bar, and lasts until it is cancelled by the next barline.

Track 28

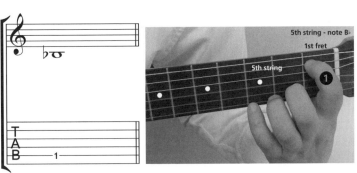

Note B♭
First finger, 1st fret
5th string

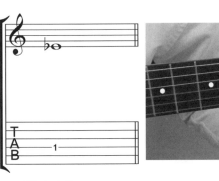

Note E♭
First finger, 1st fret
4th string

Track 29-30 *Twang!*

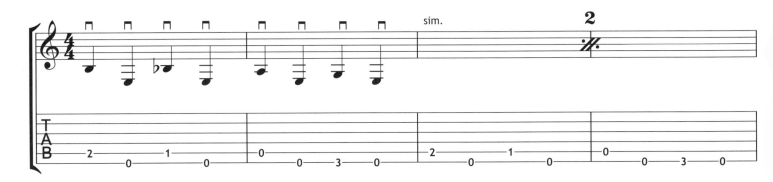

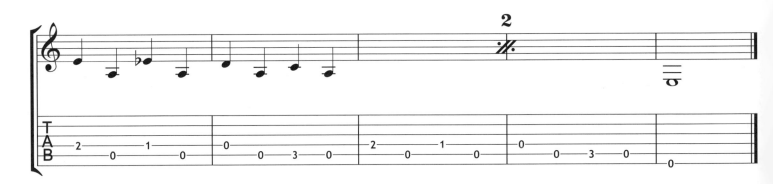

Track 31-32 *On The Edge*

Try playing the whole piece with down-strokes to create a powerful 'twangy' effect. Remember, wherever a rest symbol occurs, stop the sound of the strings with a palm mute then remove the palm mute to play the next note.

The effect of a sharp sign '♯' or flat sign '♭' may be cancelled later in the same bar by a natural sign '♮'. In bar 10 a natural sign is enclosed in brackets (♮) as a reminder that the flat sign in bar 9 has been cancelled by the barline. It is called a courtesy natural. There is a count-in of eight bars for this piece. Listen for the eight footsteps that count-in the main version on track 32.

Anacrusis

Occasionally a melody will start with an incomplete bar called an **anacrusis** (or pick-up bar).

The note values that are missing from the pick-up bar are generally the same length as the final bar of the piece. In this way, a performer could choose to 'loop' back to the start of the melody and continue playing without missing a beat.

For example the anacrusis of 'Christmas Chimes' is one beat long. The last bar is three beats long. When added together the **one beat** of the anacrusis plus the **three beats** of the last bar total the **four beats** of a full bar.

Track 33-34 *Christmas Chimes*

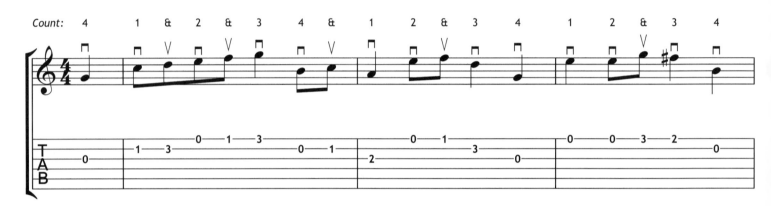

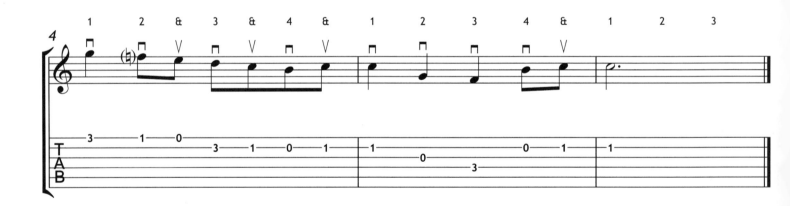

POWER CHORDS — E5, A5 AND D5*

Track 35

E5 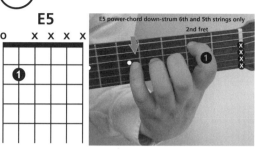 **A5** 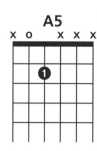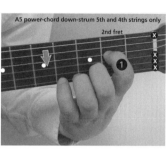 **D5**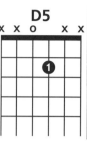

Find the finger positions for these power chords from the chord boxes above.
The 'hard', raw sound they produce is often used in rock music.

The chant 'Live It Up!' will give you some practice changing between them.

Track 36-37 *Live It Up! Chant*

play 4 times through

	Live it	up!	Live it	up!	People	everywhere	out in the	open air.	Live it
	up!	Live it	up!	When you have	time to spare and	you're with-	out a care.	Live it
	up!	Live it	up!	People	everywhere	out in the	open air.	Live it
	up!	Live it	up!	People	everywhere	out in the	open air.	Live it up!

The Palm-Muting Technique as a Strumming effect

Apply a palm mute just lightly enough so that
when the strings are strummed, they sound
muted (listen to the CD demonstration to hear
what is meant).

If the sound is too muted then move your palm
further onto the bridge (so that it touches less of
the string).

Try this exercise using down-strums with a lightly
applied palm mute.

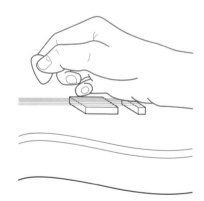

Track 38

Lightly applied
palm mute

> * The chord-symbol **'E5'** is an abbreviation of the term **E (omit 3rd)**, which means
> that the chord does not contain the 3rd degree of the scale of E Major (i.e. the
> note G♯). Likewise 'A5' means omit the C♯ and 'D5' means omit the F♯. Omitting
> the 3rd gives the chord a more powerful sound – hence the term 'power chord'.

The 'Twelve-Bar' Blues

The most famous Blues song-form is called the 'Twelve Bar' blues because the chord-sequence lasts 12 bars before being repeated. You will need to learn the following chords and riffs to start playing the Blues.*

POWER CHORDS   E6, A6 AND D6

All of these power chords are played in second position (i.e. first finger on the 2nd fret, second finger on 3rd fret etc...). When they are used together they create a classic Blues backing riff. There are three riffs to learn; they are similar but played on different strings.

To create an authentic 'blues sound' play these riffs with down-strokes using a lightly-applied palm-mute strumming effect.

Track 39

E⁵

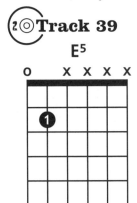

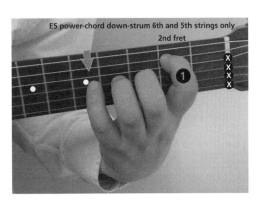

E6

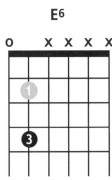

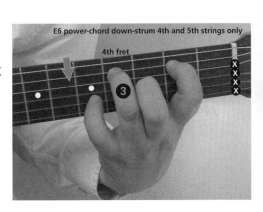

Track 40

Keep your first finger on the 5th string 2nd fret as you play the E5 – E6 Riff.

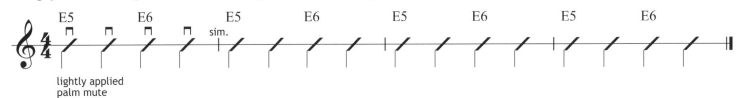

lightly applied palm mute

Track 41

A⁵

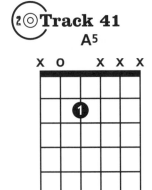

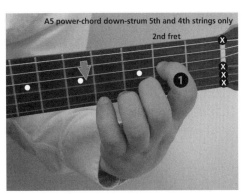

A⁶

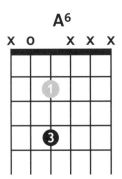

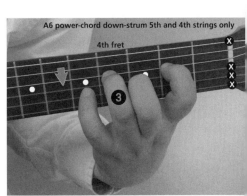

Track 42

Keep your first finger on the 4th string 2nd fret as you play the A5 – A6 Riff.

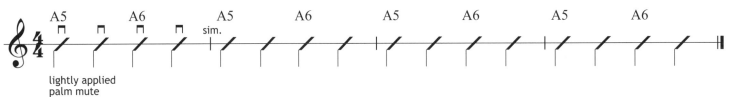

lightly applied palm mute

66

* A 'riff' is a musical phrase which may be repeated (or looped) to provide an accompaniment to a vocal line or guitar solo.

Track 43

The note 'B' – the **open 2nd string** can also be played on the **3rd string** at the **4th fret** which is much more convenient when playing the D6 power chord. Your left-hand fingers are in second position so use your third finger on the 'B'.

D5

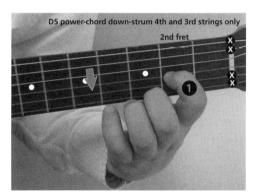

D6

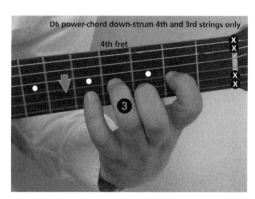

Track 44

Keep your first finger on the 3rd string 2nd fret as you play the D5 – D6 Riff.

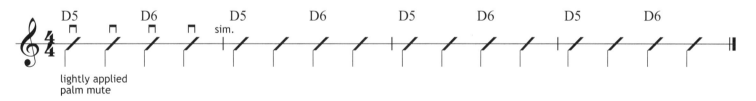

lightly applied palm mute

---

† There are many instances where the same note occurs at different places on the fretboard (see the Guitar Fretboard and Corresponding Notation Chart on page 117).

'Broad Street Stomp' uses the same riffs you learned on page 66.

Play this piece with down-strokes using the palm-muting technique throughout. The piece is demonstrated on the CD.

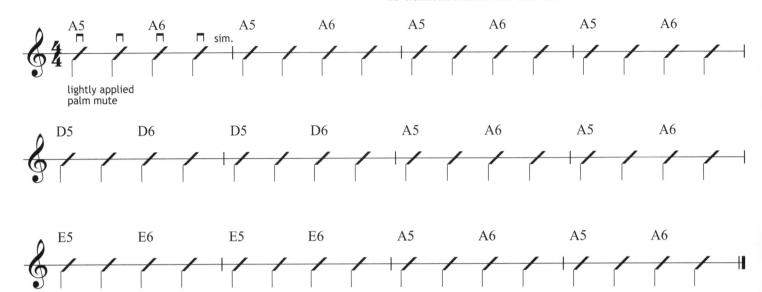

lightly applied
palm mute

Track 47-48 *Wake Up!*

'Wake Up!' should be played with down-strokes throughout.*

Take note of the instructions: palm mute and open strum shown below the music.

For example:
Play bars 1 to 5 with a lightly-applied 'palm mute'.

Play bar 6 with a normal strum (where the strings are allowed to ring-on).

Listen to the CD demonstration to hear what is meant.

Use 'Wake Up!' to practise changing between these two right-hand techniques.

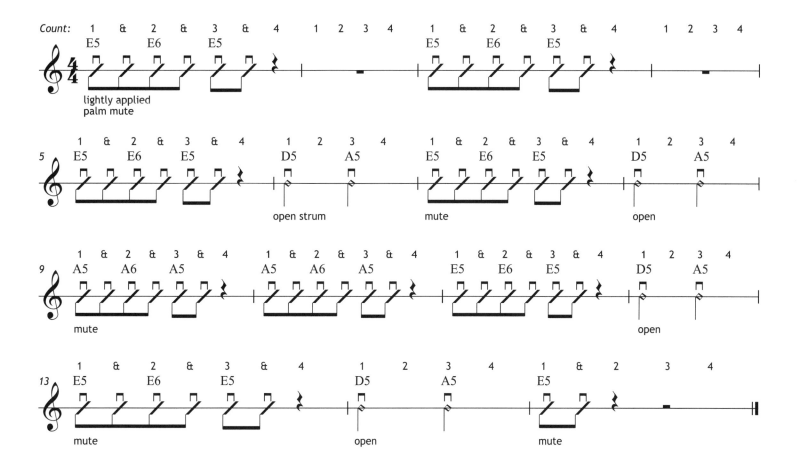

* This is an exception to the 'up-strokes on an up-beat' rule. It is easier because you are striking two strings simultaneously.

'Walk A Mile In His Shoes' should be played with down-strokes using a lightly-applied palm mute. The instruction 'With Swing' means play the eighth-notes with a 'swing' feel. A good example of a swing type feel is the nursery rhyme 'Humpty Dumpty', by contrast 'Jingle Bells' has a more 'square' or 'straight' feel.*

Listen to the CD demonstration to hear what is meant.

With swing

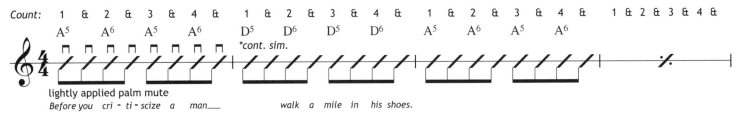

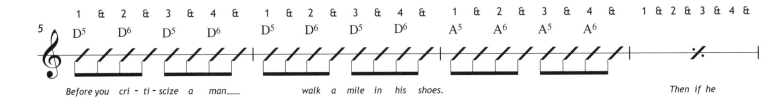

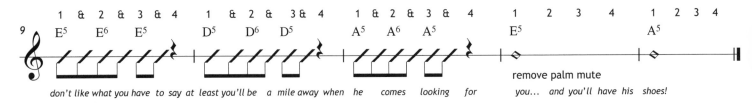

*In this context *cont. sim.* means: Continue with similar right-hand plectrum strokes throughout the piece.

*A Swing or Shuffle rhythm is sometimes shown in a time signature of $\frac{12}{8}$.

Often it can be clearer to notate in $\frac{4}{4}$ with the instruction 'With Swing' or 'Shuffle' etc. Another way to convey this feel is to denote the eighth-notes are to have a triplet feel, and is shown like this:

Rock 'n' Roll

Rock 'n' Roll uses another variation of these versatile riffs. Notice that the left-hand finger movements for the riffs are slightly different to the ones used in the earlier pieces. Also note that you play just the A5 power chord throughout bar 4 (not the A5, A6 riff).

Use the palm-muting technique with down-strokes. Remember to observe the rests, especially in bars 1, 2 and 3.

The piece is demonstrated on the CD.

Track 51-52 *Rock 'n' Roll*

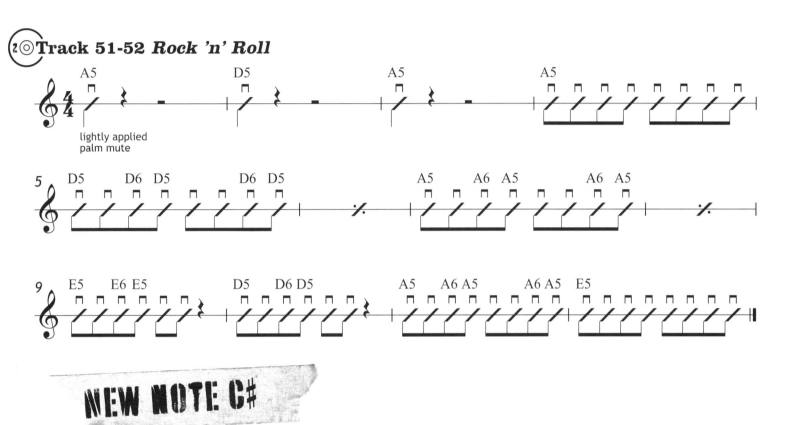

lightly applied
palm mute

Track 53

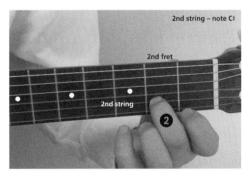

2nd string – note C♯

2nd fret

2nd string

Note C♯
Second Finger, 2nd Fret
2nd string

You will need the note C♯ on the 2nd string, 2nd fret for the chord of A7 shown on the next page.

E7 AND A7 CHORDS

Track 54

Find the finger positions for A7 and E7 from the chord boxes.

E7 uses all six strings whereas A7 uses just five.

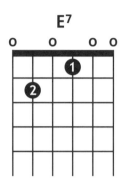

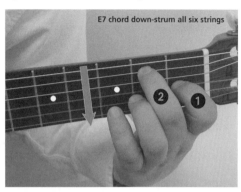

E7 chord down-strum all six strings

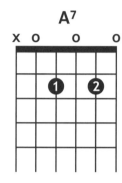

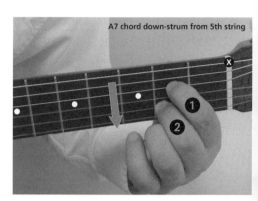

A7 chord down-strum from 5th string

Track 55-56 *Fast Lane*

play 7 times through

Track 57 The E Major chord

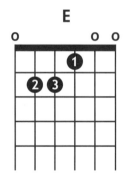

E chord down-strum all six strings

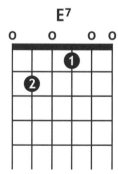

E7 chord down-strum all six strings

The E Major chord may be abbreviated to E. The finger positions are similar to E7 but with the addition of the third finger (see chord box).

So to change from E to E7, simply remove your third finger.

Track 58

Now try this exercise.

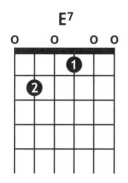
E⁷

o   o   o   o

E7 chord down-strum all six strings

D⁷

x   x   o

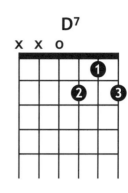

D7 chord down-strum from 4th string

Reminder of E7 and D7 chords

When changing between E7 and D7 notice that your first and second fingers form a similar shape for both chords (but on different strings).

Mo' Town

Play bars 1 to 8 with a down-strum using a lightly-applied palm-mute. In bar 9 remove the palm mute, in bar 10 ensure you strum just the four strings needed for the D7 chord.

Then re-apply the palm mute for bars 11 and 12.

E7 to **D7** change.

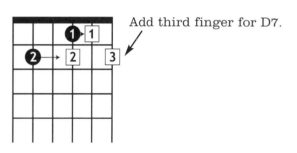

Add third finger for D7.

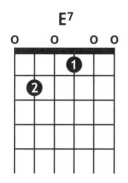
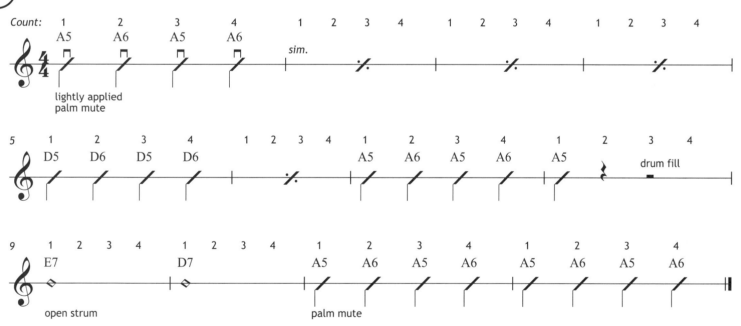

Track 62

The chord of **A Major** is similar to the **A5 power chord** and **D Major** is similar to the **D5 power chord**. To form the chord of 'A' start with the A5 chord, then add your second and third fingers as shown in the chord box.* Form the chord of 'D' in a similar way.

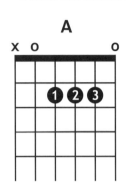
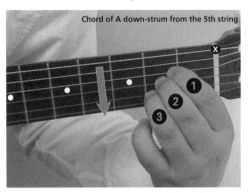

Chord of A down-strum from the 5th string

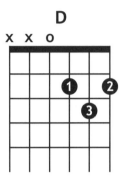
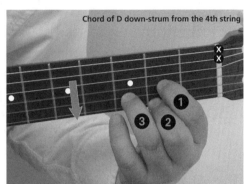

Chord of D down-strum from the 4th string

When changing from A to D, notice that your third finger remains on the 2nd string but slides from the 2nd fret to 3rd fret, then add the remaining fingers.

To change back to the A chord, reverse the process.

Now try the exercise shown below.

A to **D** change.

Slide the third finger one fret towards you.

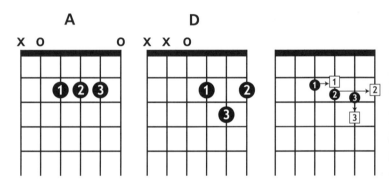

Track 63

Track 64 *Down-strum*

A down-strum is indicated by the symbol ⊓.

It should start on the thickest (lowest) string of the chord and then proceed downwards (**towards** the floor).

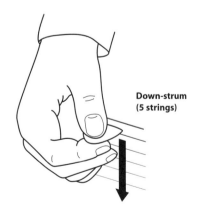

Down-strum (5 strings)

Up-strum

An up-strum is indicated by the symbol ⋁.

It should start on the thinnest (highest) string of the chord and then proceed upwards (**away** from the floor).

You don't have to strum all the strings for an up-strum, the thinnest three or four will be enough to create the rhythmic effect.

Up-strum

* An alternative fingering for the chord of A Major is shown on page 98.

Track 65

Now try this exercise. Remember that where there are no chord symbols shown above the stave, the chord from the previous bar is implied.

Track 66

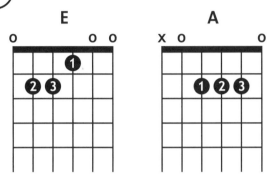

You learned the chord of E on page 72. When changing between E and A notice that your second and third fingers remain in a similar shape.

Move your second and third fingers together, then place your first finger as shown in the chord box. Practise changing back-and-forth between E and A with the exercise shown below.

E to A change.

Move your second and third fingers together (in the same shape).

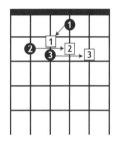

Track 67

Para Noy Ya!

Start by playing one strum per bar, until you are able
to manage the chord changes smoothly, then follow
the recommended 'strumming pattern'.

From bar 17 to the end play down-strums with a palm
mute for the power chords.

Practise the quick chord changes from bar 29 to the
end a few times until you are comfortable with the
finger movements.

Follow the music while you listen to the CD.
Check that your guitar is in tune with the CD
before playing-along.

A

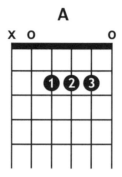

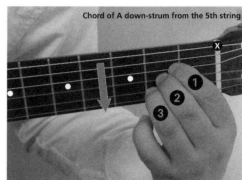

Chord of A down-strum from the 5th string

D

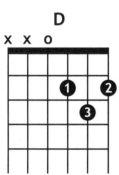

Chord of D down-strum from the 4th string

E

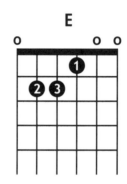

E chord down-strum all six strings

Track 68-69 *Para Noy Ya!*

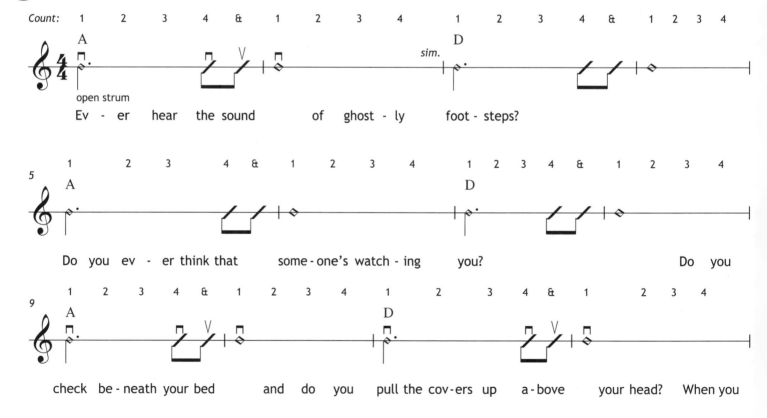

try to get to sleep do the sha-dows come for you. Just be-cause you're

Pa - ra-noid does-n't mean they ain't out to get you. Ev - 'ry

time that you close your eyes do you know for sure... that all your

toys are fast a-sleep or are they watch-ing as the moon-light starts to creep all a-

- cross the room 'till it shines up-on your door.

FULL G MAJOR AND E MINOR CHORDS

Track 70

G

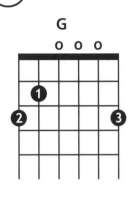

G chord (full version) down-strum all six strings

Em

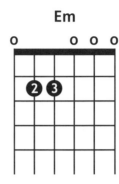

Em chord down-strum all six strings

Find the finger positions for G and E minor from the chord boxes above.

This piece is in $\frac{3}{4}$ time. Remember to mute the strings using the palm muting technique for the rests.

Track 71-72 *Dooh What?*

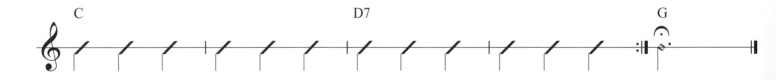

FULL G7 CHORD

There are many books available in the 'Lyric and Chord' format which is another way of representing a song (shown below).

The song is demonstrated on the CD.

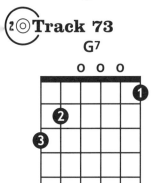

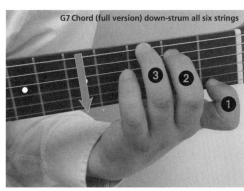

G7 Chord (full version) down-strum all six strings

C to G7 change

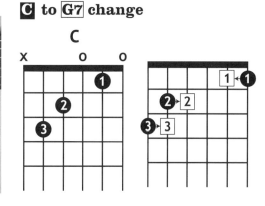

Find the finger positions for the full G7 chord from the chord box. Notice how similar the chord shapes of G7 and C are.

Play one down-strum per chord until you are familiar with the chord changes. When you are ready, try the strumming pattern shown below:

          G   D7
I asked my love to go with me

          Am   D7   G
To take a walk for a little way

          G7   C
Down beside where waters flow

          G   D7   G
Down by the banks of the O - hi - o

When you reach the last chord change to 'G' (over the letter 'o' at the end of the last line) play once through the strum pattern then play the 'G' chord and let it 'ring-on' to the end of the track. Listen to the CD demonstration to hear this played for you.

SYNCOPATED STRUMMING PATTERNS

Track 76

Syncopation is easier to hear than to explain. So, first of all, follow the notation for the straight (un-syncopated) strumming pattern shown below while you listen to the CD.

The pattern lasts one bar and is repeated.

Straight Strumming Pattern

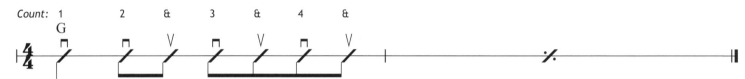

Now here is a similar strumming pattern but syncopated. Follow the notation shown below while you listen to the CD.*

Syncopated Strumming Pattern

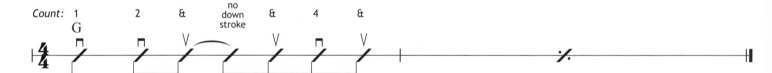

The strumming pattern has been 'syncopated' by omitting the down-strum on beat 3 of the bar (as demonstrated on the CD). This is notated using a tie.

To remind you to leave out the down-strum on the 3rd beat the '3' has been omitted from the beat count above the music thus: 1 │2 & │ & │4 & │

Follow the music for the example again, while you listen to the CD and imagine yourself strumming along – then have a go yourself.

Expect to spend a little time getting the hang of this technique; it is so widely used in pop music that it will be well worth the effort.

---

* You may find the idea of syncopation easier to grasp if you think of your plectrum-hand moving like clockwork – **down on a down-beat and up on an up-beat** (tick-tock, tick-tock). Many will find syncopation easier to 'perform' than to read about

THE D SUS2 CHORD

D suspended 2nd may be abbreviated to D sus2.

Find the finger positions for D sus2 from the chord box.

Billie and Heather (excerpt)

In the last line of the music, start by playing one strum per bar until you have mastered the chord changes.

Practise changing chord quickly from G to Em (between bars 14 and 15). Start moving your left-hand fingers as soon as you have played the last up-strum of bar 14 so you are then ready to play Em at the start of bar 15. Likewise from Em in bar 16, repeat back to G in bar 13.

Dsus²

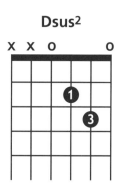

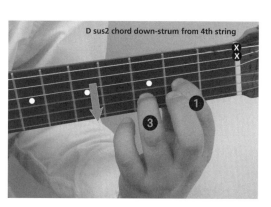

D sus2 chord down-strum from 4th string

Strumming patterns are often left to the interpretation of the guitarist, so when you are comfortable with the idea of syncopation you can either play the guide strumming pattern or experiment with your own. If it sounds right, it is right!

Track 77-78

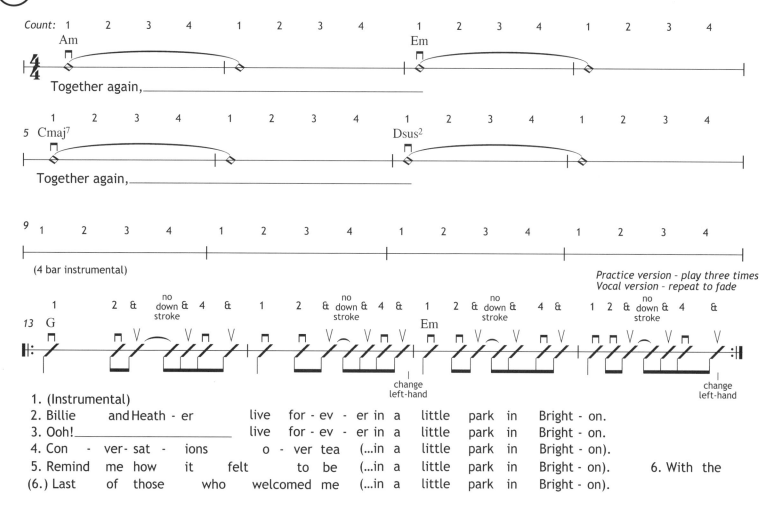

(4 bar instrumental)

Practice version – play three times
Vocal version – repeat to fade

1. (Instrumental)
2. Billie   and Heath-er   live   for - ev - er   in a   little   park   in   Bright - on.
3. Ooh!_____   live   for - ev - er   in a   little   park   in   Bright - on.
4. Con   - ver-sat - ions   o - ver tea   (...in a   little   park   in   Bright - on).
5. Remind   me how   it   felt   to   be   (...in a   little   park   in   Bright - on).   6. With the
(6.) Last   of   those   who   welcomed me   (...in a   little   park   in   Bright - on).

Track 79

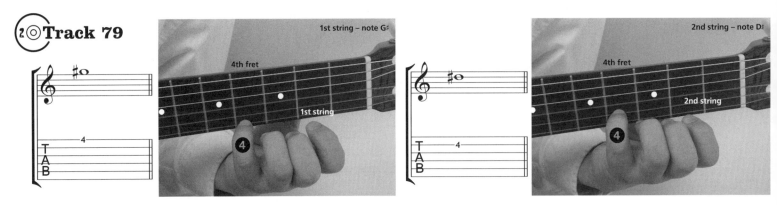

Note G♯
Fourth finger, 4th fret
1st string

Note D♯
Fourth finger, 4th fret
2nd string

Track 80-81 *Falling*

This piece will help strengthen the fourth finger of your left hand and provide you with some practice at swapping between strings with your plectrum.

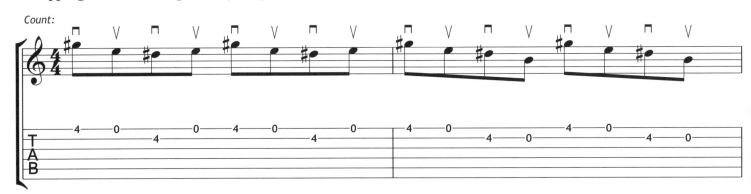

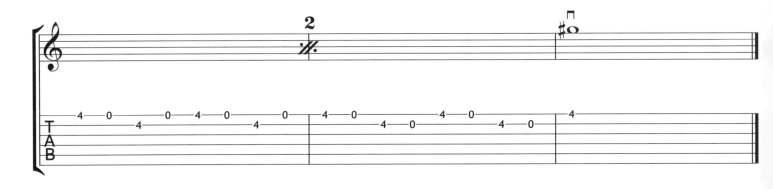

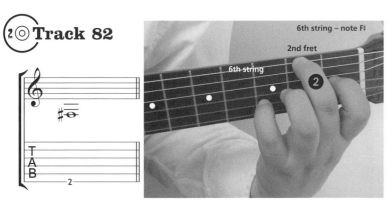

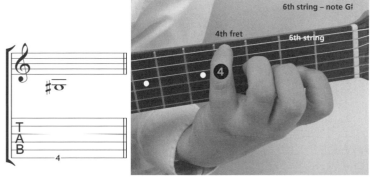

Note F♯
Second finger, 2nd fret
6th string

Note G♯
Fourth finger, 4th fret
6th string

Keep your left-hand fingers in second position throughout the piece – (use the fingerings shown in the photos below to play new notes F♯ and G♯ in second position). Wherever there's a rest, remember to stop the sound of the strings.

Practise the change between bar 4 and bar 5 slowly until the finger movements become easy.

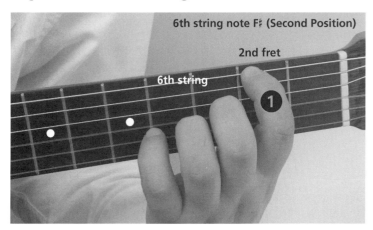

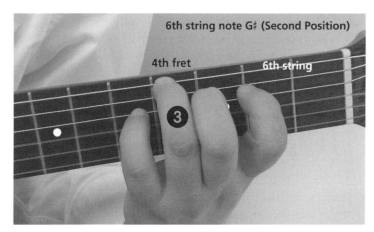

Track 83-84

Omnes...!

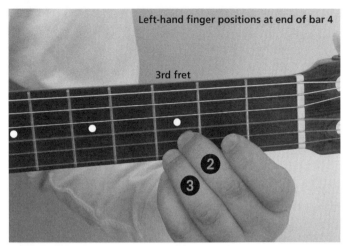

Left-hand finger positions at end of bar 4

3rd fret

end of bar 4

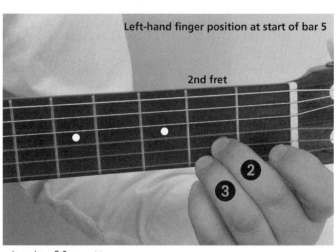

Left-hand finger position at start of bar 5

2nd fret

start of bar 5

Use plectrum down-strokes to strike the 1st and 2nd strings simultaneously throughout bars 1 to 8 as indicated in 'Omnes!'. This is an exception to the 'up-strokes on an up-beat' rule – in this context multiple down-strokes work well because they are louder and more percussive. The same exception applies to bars 23 and 24.

Notice that at the end of bar 4 you need only to slide your left-hand fingers down from the 3rd to 2nd fret – whilst keeping them in the same shape – to play bars 5, 6, 7 and 8 (this is shown in the photos above).

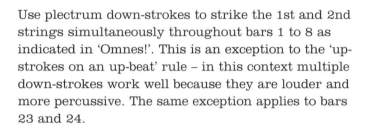

THE NATURAL SIGN ♮

Remember that the effect of a sharp symbol ♯ starts from where it appears in the bar and lasts until it is cancelled by the next barline. The effect of a sharp sign may also be cancelled later in the same bar by a 'natural' sign ♮.

You can leave your third finger on the 1st string at the 3rd fret throughout bars 1 to 4.

Now look at bar 13. When a natural sign is enclosed in brackets (♮) it is a reminder to the musician that a sharp (or flat) sign in an earlier bar has been cancelled by a barline. It is called a 'courtesy natural'. In this case it is a reminder to play C and not C♯.

Wherever a rest symbol occurs, remember to mute the strings using the palm muting technique and then remove the palm mute to play the next notes. Listen to the CD practice track.

2

Track 85-86 *Omnes...!*

* If, after a reasonable period of practice, you still find the palm mute tricky at this stage then you can play a simplified version of the first eight bars by letting the strings ring-on over the rests instead of muting them. You can always try it with palm muting later.

PREPARATORY EXERCISES FOR BLUES SOLO

Hammer-on

Listen to the exercise demonstrated on the CD.

To play bar 1, strike the open 3rd string with your plectrum.

Then (while the string is still sounding) 'Hammer' your first finger down 'on' to the 2nd fret (3rd string) to sound the next note instead of striking the string again with your plectrum. Hence the term 'hammer on'. To play bar 3 use the same hammer-on technique on the 4th string.

Practise this slowly at first until you can do it easily enough to play-along with hammer-on Exercise 1.

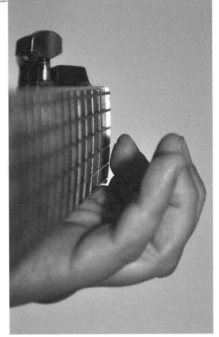 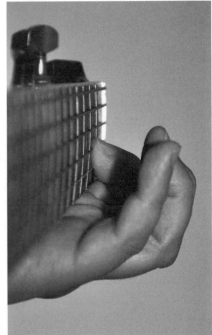

Track 87

Exercise 1

Hammer-on

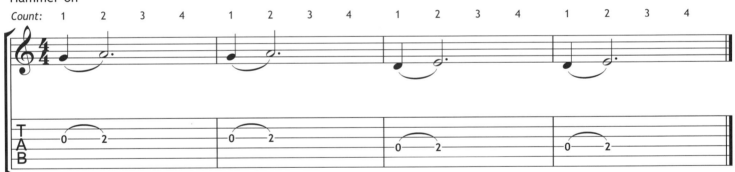

Exercise 2

This is a faster hammer-on.

Faster Hammer-on

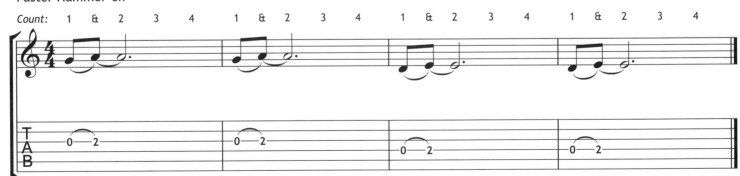

Pull-off

Before

After

Listen to the exercise demonstrated on the CD.
To play bar 1, place your first finger on the 3rd
string 2nd fret.

Strike the string and (while it is still sounding) 'Pull'
your third finger 'off' with a downwards plucking
motion to 'sound' the open 3rd string instead of
striking the string again with your plectrum.

To play bar 3 use the same pull-off technique on the
4th string.

Practise this slowly at first until you can do it easily
enough to play-along with pull-off Exercise 1.

Exercise 1

Pull-off

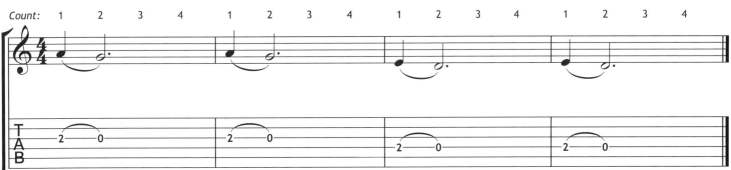

Exercise 2

Faster Pull-off

Simple String Bending

Before

During

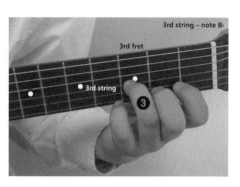

3rd string – note B♭

3rd fret

3rd string

3

New note 'B♭'
Third finger, 3rd fret
3rd string

You will need to have light gauge strings on your guitar if you want to bend them. Look at the Tab stave for bar 1 in the exercise below, the curved arrow pointing to a ½ is an instruction to bend the string so that the pitch raises ½ a tone (in this case from 'A' to 'B♭').

To play bar 1, place your first finger on the 3rd string, 2nd fret (the note 'A'). Strike the string and (while it is still sounding) gently pull the string downwards with a turning motion of the wrist. Use just enough force to raise the pitch a semitone higher so that it sounds like the note 'B♭' (which is located one fret higher on the 3rd string, 3rd fret). Then just before beat 3 (still keeping your first finger on the 2nd fret) quickly relax the downwards pressure on the 3rd string to return the pitch back to the note 'A'. Strike the 3rd string on beat 3. Follow the music while you listen to the CD demonstration.

Compare your string bend to the 'B♭' note given on the CD but don't worry if you can't bend the string far enough. When playing 'The Blues' a string bend can be near enough to the target note (in this case B♭) and still sound good even if it's a little out-of-tune.

String-bending Exercise

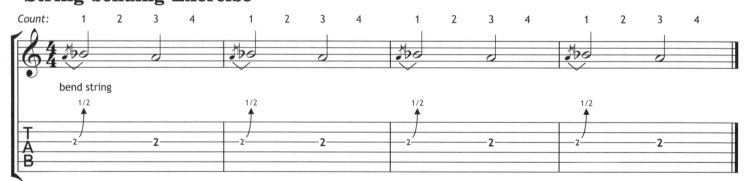

String-bend and Pull-off Exercise

The string-bend (over the first two beats) is played in the same way as the previous exercise. The pull-off is played in the same way as bar 1 of Pull-off Exercise 2.

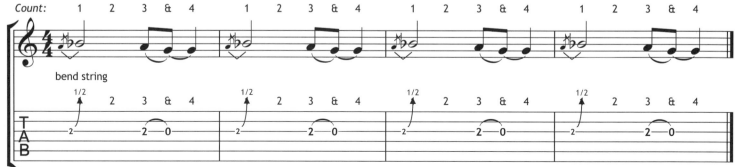

Vibrato

The symbol ∿∿∿∿∿∿∿∿ shown above a note on the stave is a vibrato instruction.
This could be described as: 'multiple stringbends performed in quick succession'.

To play bar 1, place your first finger on the 3rd string, 2nd fret (the note 'A').
Strike the string and while it is still sounding:
1. Pull the string downwards with a gentle turning motion of the wrist to raise the pitch
2. Immediately relax your downwards pressure until the pitch returns to normal.

Carry out steps 1 and 2 in rapid succession for the duration of the note over which the vibrato line is placed.
Use just enough pressure to vary the pitch of the note (you don't have to reach 'B♭').

Some guitarists like to leave a gap of a beat or two before applying vibrato to a note. When you have learned the technique you can experiment with this; it is a matter of personal taste.

Vibrato Exercise

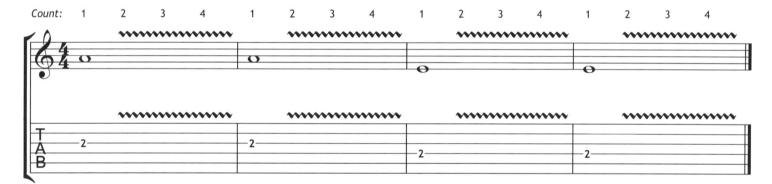

Hammer-on and Vibrato Exercise

Hammer-on and then vibrato.
It is important to aim your hammer-on finger so that it comes to rest on the string in such a way that you can pull the string downwards as described above.
In other words, aim to get a good grip with your finger.

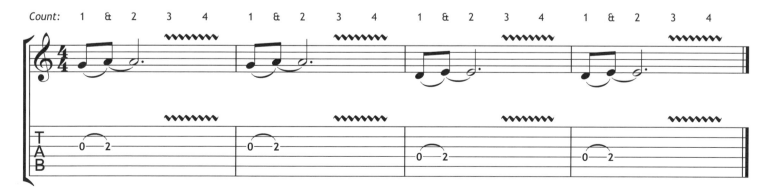

Blues Solo

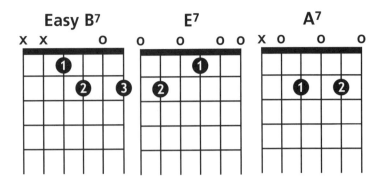

Learn the finger positions for the Easy 'B7' chord.

At the end of bar 24 the instruction 'D.C. al Fine' (pronounced Da Capo al Feenay) means that you should play (again) from the start through to the instruction 'Fine' (bar 12).

Listen to the CD demonstration while you follow the music to make sure you have understood the repeat structure.

In this piece you play a solo and then (from bar 13) chords to provide an accompaniment while another instrument plays a solo.

Finally you play the solo again to end the piece.

 **Track 91-92** *Blues Solo*

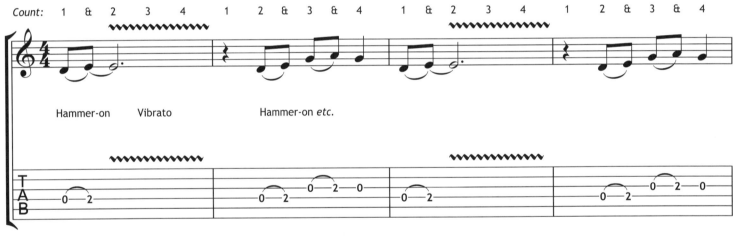

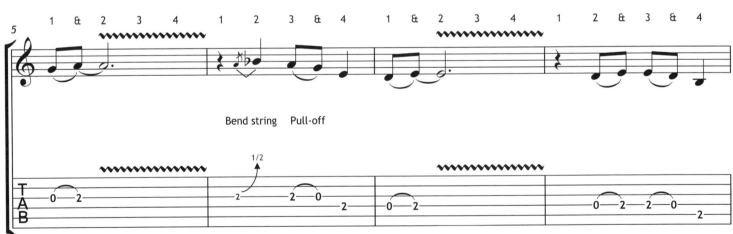

*'Fine' is Italian for 'end' and is pronounced 'feenay'.
On the second time through the piece ends at the end of bar 12

* All the notes you can play while your left-hand is in first position i.e.: frets 1 to 4 on all strings.

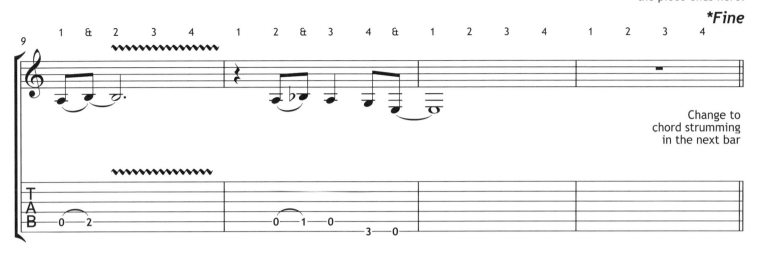

Change to
chord strumming
in the next bar

Change to chord strumming

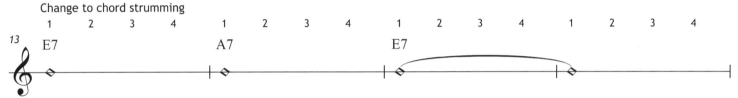

Remember the chord boxes E7 and A7

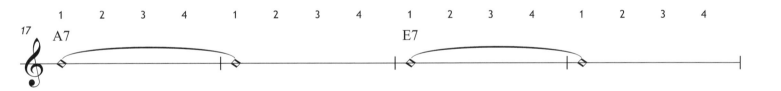

D.C. al Fine

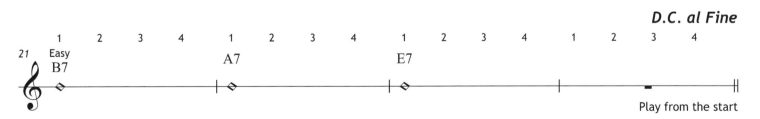

Play from the start

Change back to playing
single notes from bar 1

*Play from the start to the instruction 'Fine' at bar 12

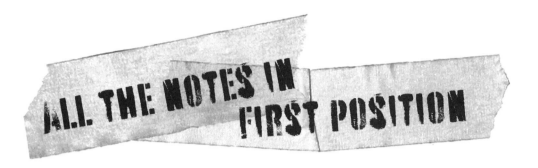

ALL THE NOTES IN FIRST POSITION

You have now covered all the notes in 'first position', these are all shown below.* The interval between each of these notes is a semitone (one fret). A scale entirely made up of semitones is called a 'chromatic scale', which can begin on any note.

* All the notes you can play while your left-hand is in first position i.e.: frets 1 to 4 on all strings.

CONGRATULATIONS!

This is the end of the tutorial section of the book. If you have played through all the songs and exercises you will have learned the rudiments of good plectrum technique and will now be able to play all the notes available in 'first position' and many of the basic chords.

A good way to proceed is to read and play as much music as you can, you should now have enough knowledge to tackle most basic guitar tab and repertoire books.

A chord dictionary is a very useful reference book to have at hand when learning new songs; as well as the book 'How To Read Music' (Wise Publications, AM986887) which explains traditional music notation in more detail.

In the last song, 'My Fearless Girlfriend' (page 96), you will use many of the techniques you have learned and the majority of students will find it challenging. The idea is to stretch your ability to the maximum – don't feel discouraged if you find it difficult to play. You have already done well to finish the book, the emphasis here is on having-a-go for fun. Before you get to this song, work through the next preparatory exercises...

Good Luck!

These are preparatory exercises for the next song (p96). You learned about syncopated strumming patterns on p80; the next song uses syncopated riffs (i.e., notes instead of chords). The rhythms and plectrum techniques are quite advanced so take your time to work through these exercises.

Track 93

Exercise 1

Listen to the CD demonstration to hear the timing.

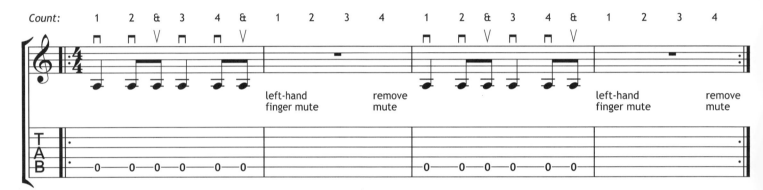

Exercise 2

This has the same rhythm as Exercise 1 but with different notes. It is identical to the riff you will play in bars 1 to 8 of the next song.

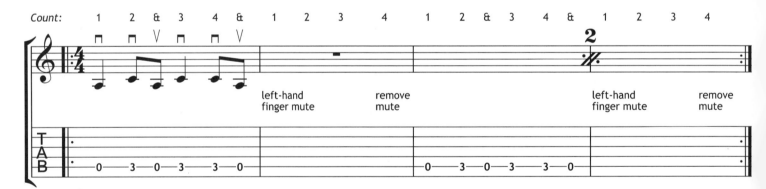

Exercise 3

This is identical to the riff you will play in bars 9 to 12 of the next song. Listen to the CD demonstration to hear the timing. Pay special attention to the rhythm and plectrum strokes from the end of bar 2.

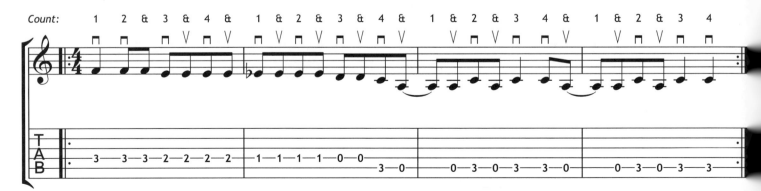

Exercise 4

This is identical to the riff you will play in bars 13 to 16 of the next song. Listen to the CD demonstration. Practise the manoeuvre of playing the last three notes followed by a 'palm mute' until you can do it easily.

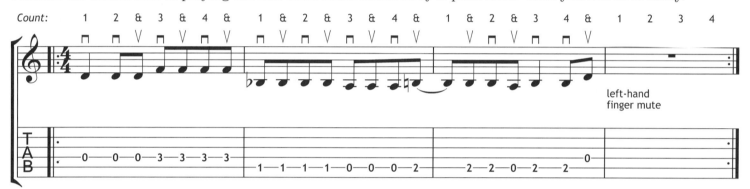

Exercise 5

This exercise uses the same syncopated rhythm you learned on p80. It is identical to the riff you will play in bars 17 to 20 of the next song. The plectrum strokes in bars 1 and 2 will require careful practice. This is demonstrated on the CD.

Exercise 6

This is identical to the riff you will play in bars 33 to 36 of the next song. Play along using down-strokes throughout.

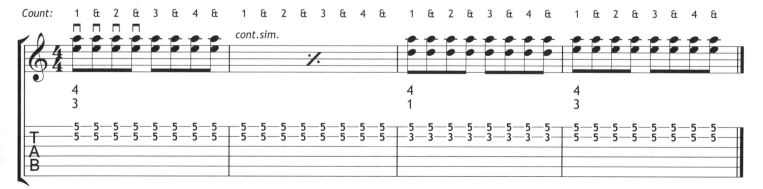

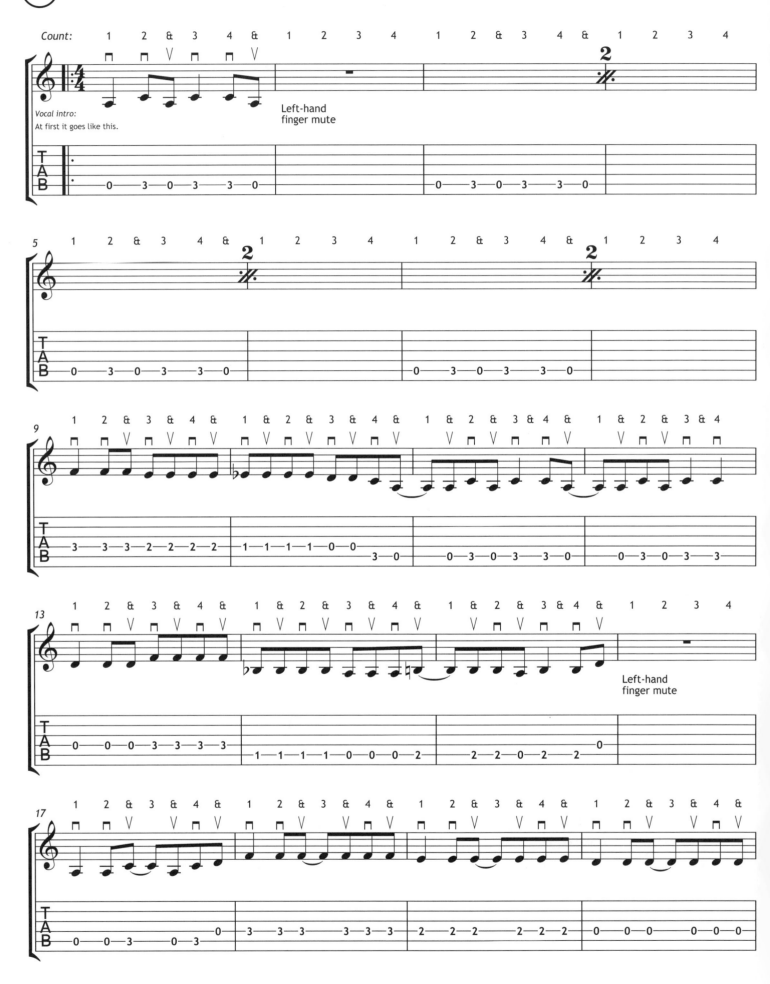

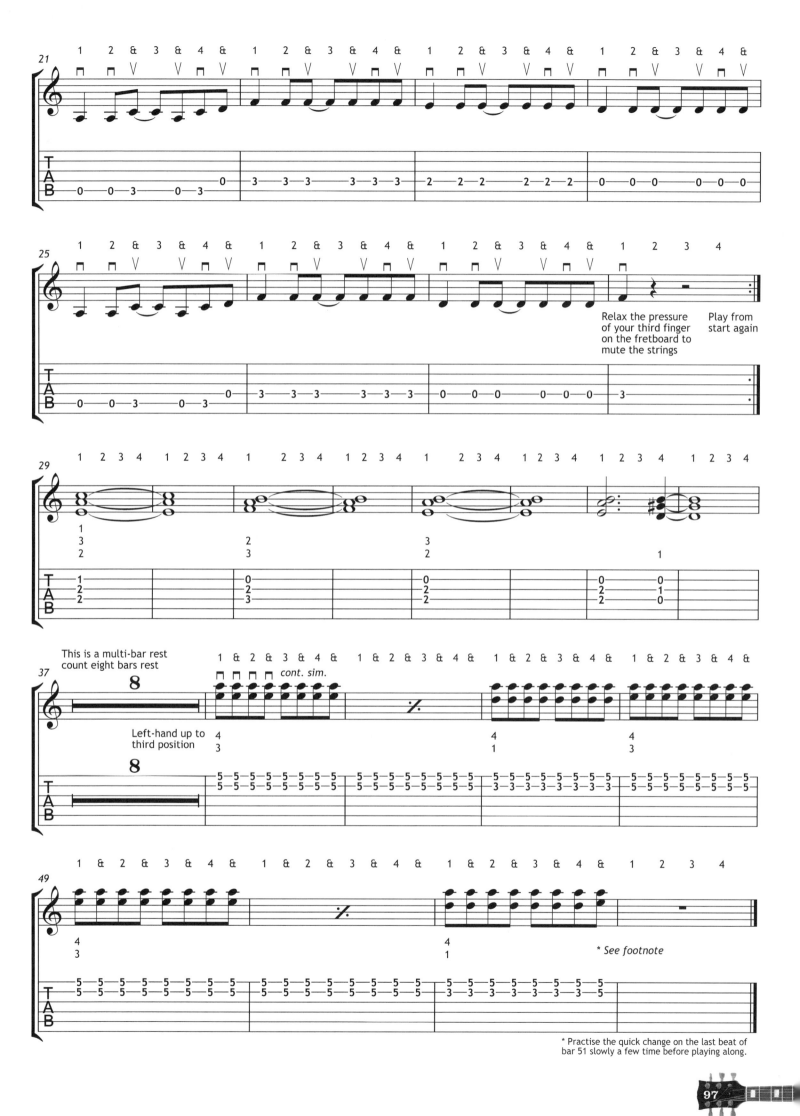

Relax the pressure of your third finger on the fretboard to mute the strings

Play from start again

This is a multi-bar rest count eight bars rest

Left-hand up to third position

cont. sim.

* See footnote

* Practise the quick change on the last beat of bar 51 slowly a few time before playing along.

CHORD CHART

Here are the chords you have learned in the book.

Here is an alternative fingering for the chord of 'A' Major.

Easy Chords

Easy C
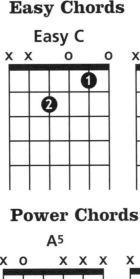

Easy G
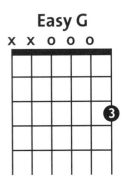

Easy G^7
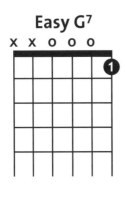

A
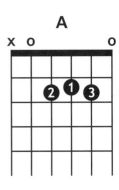

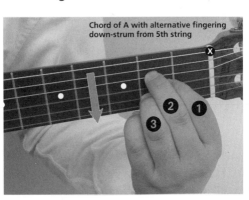

Chord of A with alternative fingering down-strum from 5th string

Power Chords

A^5
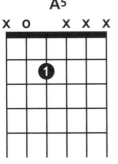

A^6
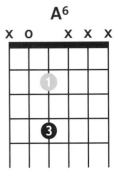

D^5
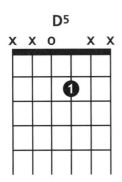

D^6
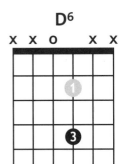

E^5
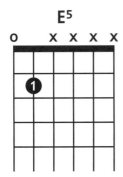

E^6
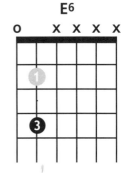

Full Chords

A
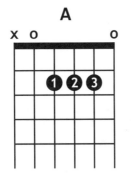

Am
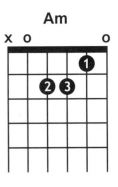

A^7
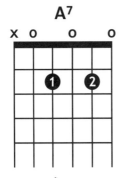

Asus^2
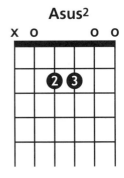

C
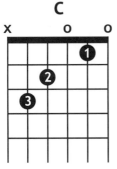

Easy B^7
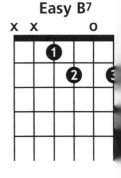

Cmaj^7
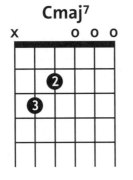

D
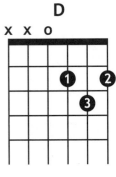

D^7
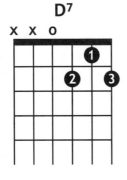

Dsus^2
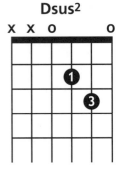

Dm
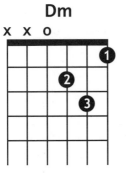

Dm^6

E
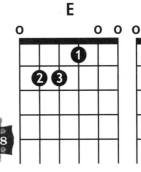

Em
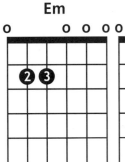

E^7
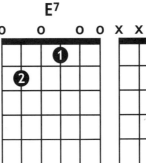

F Maj^7
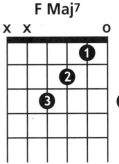

G
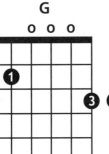

G^7
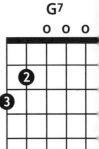

OTHER METHODS OF TUNING

Tuning to a Keyboard

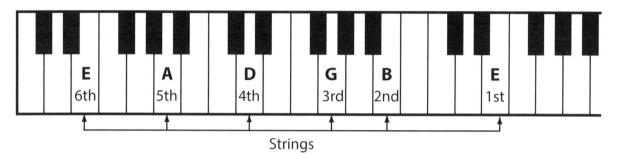

Strings

Above shows the positions on a keyboard where you would find the notes to tune your guitar to.
Play the corresponding note on the keyboard while you tune the string to the correct pitch.

Using an Electronic Tuner

Some electronic tuners have a socket you can plug your guitar lead straight into, some may only have a built-in microphone, while others have both.

Relative Tuning

Tune one string at a time starting from the low E or 6th string.
Estimate the pitch of the 6th string as near to 'E' as possible.

Hold-down and play the:
5th fret of the E (6th) string; tune the open 5th string to that pitch.
5th fret of the A (5th) string; tune the open 4th string to that pitch.
5th fret of the D (4th) string; tune the open 3rd string to that pitch.
4th fret of the G (3rd) string; tune the open 2nd string to that pitch.
5th fret of the B (2nd) string; tune the open 1st string to that pitch.

This is a great method for making sure the guitar is in tune with 'itself', but you may run into difficulties when playing with others if they have tuned using a tuner or you are playing with an instrument that can't change its tuning easily (like a keyboard or piano).

Whichever method you use, you may need to repeat the procedure a few times to get all the strings sounding just right. This has to do with the guitar adjusting to the new tension of the strings. Remember that air temperature can dramatically affect the guitar's ability to stay in tune.

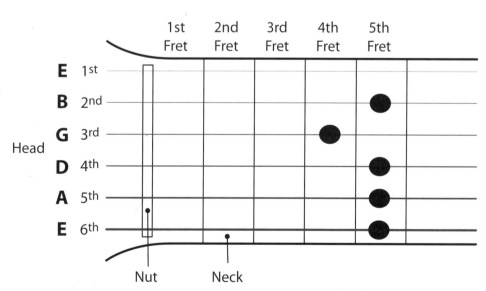

INTERVALS, SCALES AND KEY SIGNATURES

In traditional music notation, the word 'interval' describes the pitch distance between two notes. The interval of a 'tone' is equivalent to the distance of two frets on the guitar, the interval of a 'semi-tone' is equivalent to the distance of one fret. The 'Major' scale has a pattern of intervals (or gaps) between each note. The scale of C Major starts from C and comprises the letter-note names C, D, E, F, G, A, B and C, it does not need any sharps or flats. Here is the scale of 'C' Major:

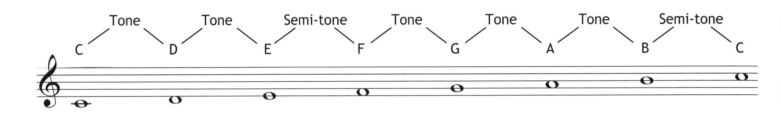

The example below starts on G and comprises the notes G, A, B, C, D, E, F and G but it is not the scale of G major. Try playing it and you may hear that the note 'F' sounds out of place.

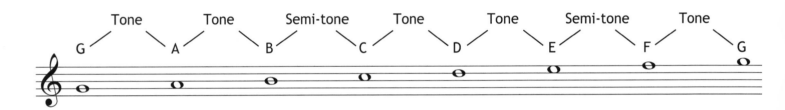

In order to maintain the pattern of intervals for the Major Scale (Tone, Tone, Semi-tone, Tone, Tone, Tone, Semi-tone, as shown above for C Major), all the 'F' notes need to be raised to 'F♯'. Therefore the key signature of 'G Major' comprises an 'F♯'. When the 'G Major' key signature is added to the start of the example, it becomes the scale of G major.

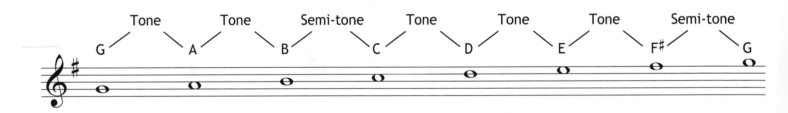

* See Guitar fretboard and corresponding music notation chart on page 117.

TROUBLESHOOTING

Use this page to help diagnose any difficulties you may encounter.

If your guitar sounds **out of tune** with the CD or unpleasant to the ear:

- Make sure that the guitar is properly tuned. Check the strings against the tuning tones (tracks 3 to 8).

- Check that the strings are not too old and worn to sound clearly. Old and worn strings sound dull and are difficult to tune. If you are having difficulty changing strings, ask if your local music shop offers this service.

If you hear a **loud buzzing sound** each time you play the **open strings**:

- Make sure that the string ends are not so long that they 'buzz' against the wood of the guitar. Check the condition of the lower strings, the thin metal 'windings' can become frayed when they are too old and worn.

- If you have carried out the above checks but they haven't cured the problem, then the guitar may need to be set-up or repaired by a guitar technician. Your local music shop may offer this service.

If you hear a **buzzing sound** when you use your **left-hand fingers** to hold down the strings on the fretboard:

- Are you pressing the string down firmly against the fretboard?

- Are your left-hand fingernails short enough?

- Are you pressing the string down close enough to the metal fret-wire to avoid a buzzing sound? Look at the diagram labelled 'Correct Position'.

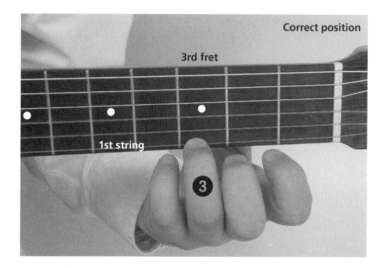

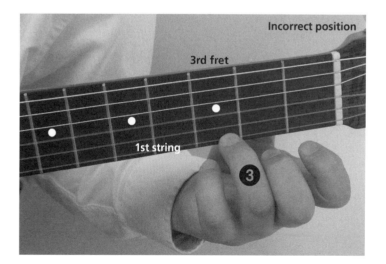

BASIC QUIZ

Fill in the labels describing the features of the guitar.

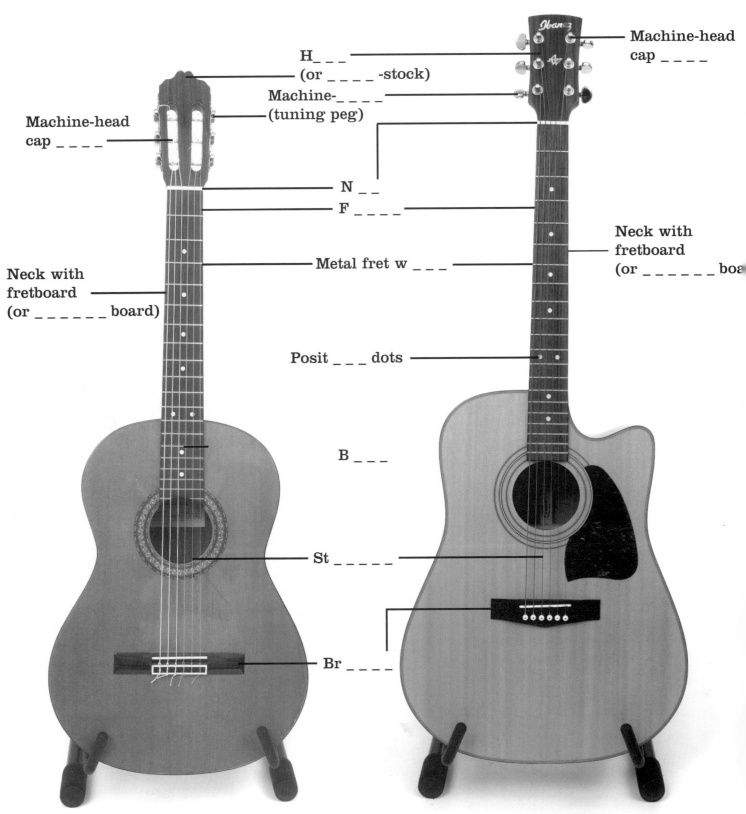

Machine-head cap _ _ _ _

H_ _ _
(or _ _ _ _ -stock)

Machine-_ _ _ _
(tuning peg)

N _ _

F _ _ _ _

Metal fret w _ _ _

Posit _ _ _ dots

B _ _ _

St _ _ _ _ _

Br _ _ _ _

Machine-head cap _ _ _ _

Machine-head cap _ _ _ _

Neck with fretboard (or _ _ _ _ _ _ board)

Neck with fretboard (or _ _ _ _ _ _ boa

Acoustic nylon-string guitar

Acoustic steel-string guitar

Fill in the labels describing the features of the electric guitar.

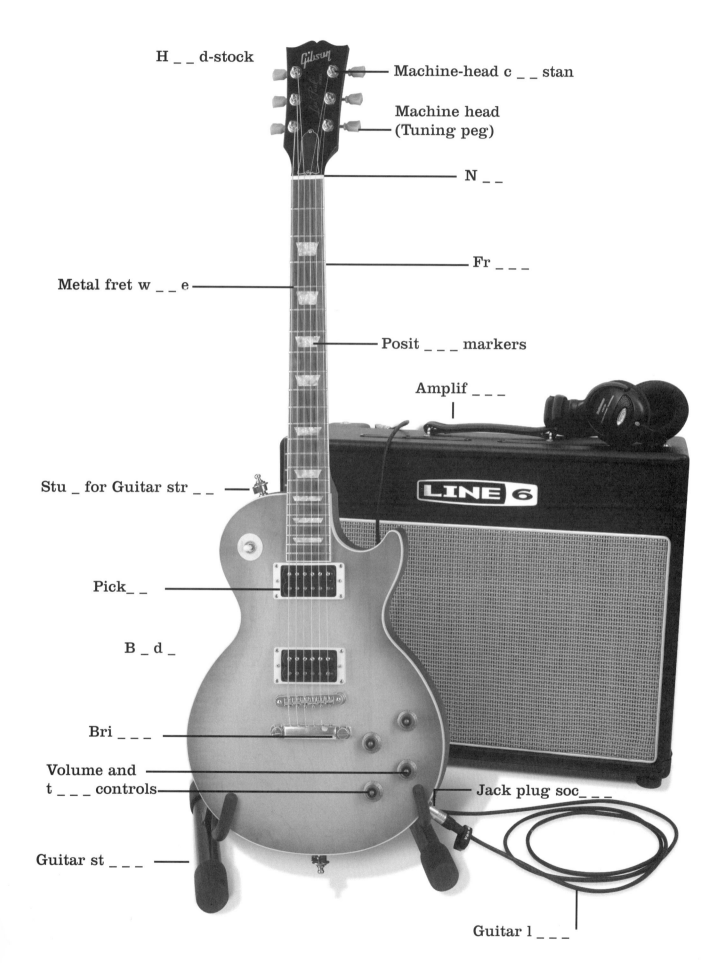

H _ _ d-stock

Machine-head c _ _ stan

Machine head
(Tuning peg)

N _ _

Fr _ _ _

Metal fret w _ _ e

Posit _ _ _ markers

Amplif _ _ _

Stu _ for Guitar str _ _

Pick_ _

B _ d _

Bri _ _ _

Volume and
t _ _ _ controls

Jack plug soc_ _ _

Guitar st _ _ _

Guitar l _ _ _

Complete the following sentences by filling in the missing words or symbols.

Right-Hand Notation

Down-strokes are indicated by the symbol: ____

A down-stroke should start on the upper side of the string and then proceed _ _ _ _ _ _ _ _ (towards the floor).

Label the machine-heads with the letter-note names corresponding to the strings.

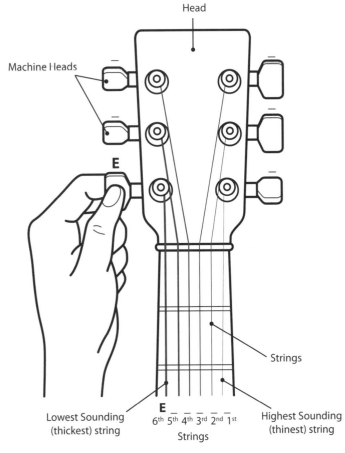

Head

Machine Heads

E

Strings

Lowest Sounding (thickest) string

E
6th 5th 4th 3rd 2nd 1st
Strings

Highest Sounding (thinest) string

Reading Music

Traditional Music Notation is written on five parallel lines called a _ _ _ _ _ (or a staff). Musical tones are represented by _ _ _ _ _ written on the stave.

The _ _ _ _ _ of a note describes how high or low it sounds.

Add the 'letter names' of the notes to the corresponding lines and spaces.

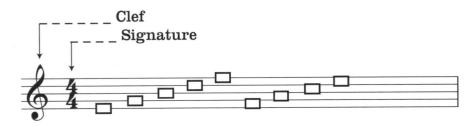

_ _ _ _ _ _ **Clef**
_ _ _ _ _ **Signature**

Rhythm

The stave is separated into b _ _ _ (or **measures**) by vertical lines called **bar li** _ _ _.

Each bar has a fixed number of **beats** according to the **Ti _ _ signature** of the music.

A **beat** may be described as the natural foot-tapping rhythm of a piece of music. A time signature appears at the beginning of most music and consists of two numbers.

The **top number** denotes the number of **b _ _ _ _** in each bar.

The **lower number** denotes the value of a **b _ _ _**.

For example:
The time signature $\frac{4}{4}$ describes four beats in a bar, each beat with the value of a quarter-note (as shown below). The four quarter-notes add up to a whole-note. Most rock and pop pieces have four beats in a bar.

Notes have a time value that corresponds to the beat.

Note Values:
o a **whole-note** (or semibreve) lasts **f _ _ r beats.**

a **h _ _ _ -note** (or **m _ _ _ m**) lasts _ _ _ **beats.**

a **qu _ _ _ _ _ -note** (or **cr _ _ _ _ _ t**) lasts _ _ _ **beat.**

A piece of music in $\frac{4}{4}$ time may contain notes in any combination of time value, provided the total (time value) per bar adds up to one **wh _ _ _ -note**, also known as a (**s _ _ _ br _ _ _**).

The Left Hand

Add the correct finger numbers to the diagram of the left hand.

Most often you will use your:

First finger on the 1st fret.

S_ _ _ _ _ finger on the 2nd fret.

T _ _ _ _ finger on the 3rd fret and

F _ _ _ _ _ finger on the 4th fret.

The Guitar Tablature stave

The guitar tablature stave has six lines, each representing a **st _ _ _ _** on the guitar.

Add the string numbers and corresponding letter-note names to the lines of the Tab stave.

A number shown on a tablature line indicates the **f _ _ _** number on which your finger should be placed to hold down (or 'stop') the corresponding **st _ _ _ _** .

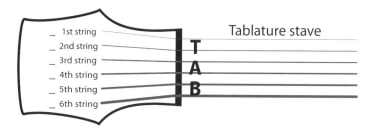

Thus: **2** indicates the **2nd fret** and **3** indicates the **_ rd** fret etc.

A zero (0) indicates that the string should be played **op _ _** or unstopped.

1ST STRING QUIZ

These notes are to be played on the 1st string. Add the corresponding fret numbers for each note to the Tab stave and then fill-in their letter-names on the spaces shown below.

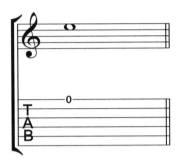

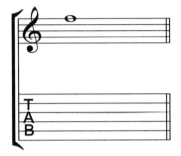

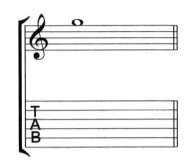

Note E
Open
1st string

Note _
First finger, 1st fret
1st string

Note _
Third finger, 3rd fret
1st string

A dot placed to the right of a note increases its time value by a **h _ _ f** .

Complete the 'beat count' over the music stave and then add the letter name corresponding to each note. Draw a 'final barline' at the end of the last bar.

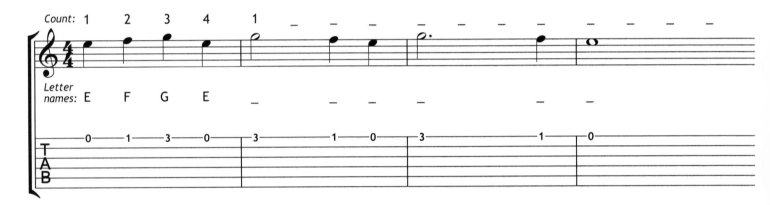

2ND STRING QUIZ

Add the corresponding fret numbers for each note to the Tab stave and fill in their letter names on the spaces shown below.

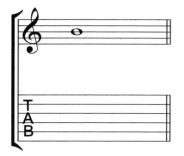

Note B
Open
2nd string

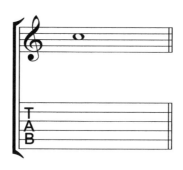

Note _
First finger, 1st fret
2nd string

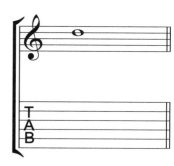

Note _
Third finger, 3rd fret
2nd string

The following symbols are **r _ _ _ _ t** signs: $\|$:   :$\|$

The music between these two symbols should be played **tw _ _ _** unless otherwise specified.
If the left-hand symbol does not appear, the player should go back to the **st _ _ _** of the piece.

Add the 'beat count' and then add the letter name for each note below.

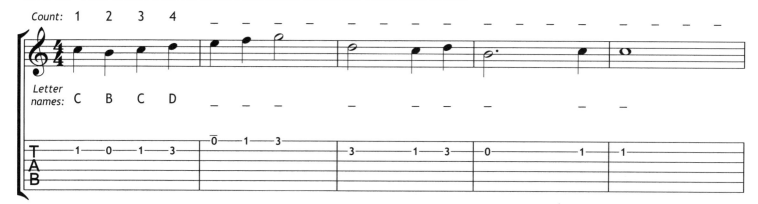

A curved line joining notes of the same pitch is called a **t _ _** .

Fill-in the missing time values below.

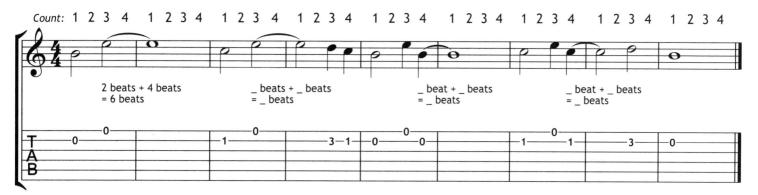

The symbol ⌒ shown over a note (or chord) is called a **fer _ _ _ _**. It means hold the note (or chord) for as **l _ _ g** as you wish or until it fades out naturally.

3RD STRING QUIZ

Add the corresponding fret numbers for each note to the Tab stave and fill in their letter names on the spaces shown below.

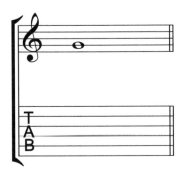

Note _
Open
3rd string

Note _
Second finger, 2nd fret
3rd string

The note 'G' on the open 3rd string is separated from the note 'G' on the 1st string 3rd fret by an interval known as an **oc _ _ _ _**.

This symbol ⁄⁄ means **re _ _ _ _** the preceding bar. It is called a **measure repeat sign** (or bar repeat sign).

Add the missing stems to all of the notes. Any notes higher than the 'B' in the stave should have the

downward stems, notes below the 'B' should have upward stems (the 'B' itself can have a stem in either direction).

Then add the missing barlines and complete the 'beat count' above the stave.

Finally add the letter names corresponding to each note.

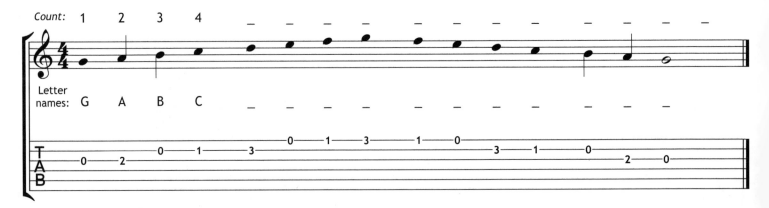

This piece is in $\frac{3}{4}$. Fill in the beat count, then add the letter names corresponding to each note.

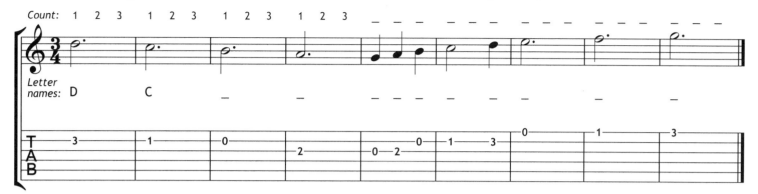

Add the finger and fret numbers to the labels on this picture of the left hand in 2nd position.

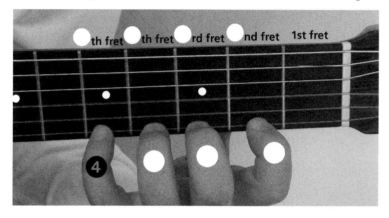

A rest denotes a period of **sil _ _ _ _**, when the musician plays nothing.

Notes and rests have a time value that corresponds to the beat.

o   a **whole-note** (or **semibreve**) lasts **f _ _ _ beats**.

♩   a **h _ _ _ -note** (or **m _ _ _ _**) lasts **t _ _ beats**.

♪   a **q _ _ _ _ _ _ _ -note** (or **c _ _ _ _ _ _ _ _**) lasts **o _ _ beat**.

4TH STRING QUIZ

Add the corresponding fret numbers for each note to the Tab stave and fill in their letter names on the spaces shown below.

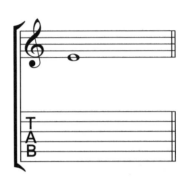

Note _
Open
4th string

Note _
Second finger, 2nd fret
4th string

Note _
Third finger, 3rd fret
4th string

Use the two empty staves to write out this music in full (i.e. without using the repeat signs). It doesn't matter if you haven't written down any music before; just copy the shapes of the notes and their stems as neatly as you can. Take care to write the note heads on the correct line or in the correct space. The stems should be drawn at right angles to the stave, and attached to the note heads. Make sure the stems follow the same direction as the original. Use a pencil so that you can correct any mistakes easily.

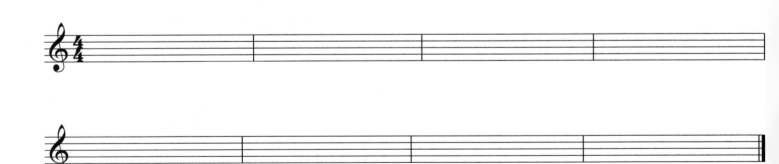

The symbol ♯ is a s _ _ _ p sign. When it is placed to the left of a note it raises the pitch of that note by h _ _ f a tone (or _ fret). Its effect lasts for o _ _ bar.

This symbol ♮ is a n _ _ _ _ al sign which can cancel the effect of a sharp sign later in the same bar. When a natural sign is enclosed in brackets (♮) it is included as a reminder to the musician that a sharp sign in an earlier bar has been cancelled by a barline. It is called a 'cou _ _ _ sy natural'.

The symbol 2 ✕ means repeat the preceding t _ _ bars.

The symbol 4 ✕ means repeat the preceding f _ _ _ bars.

The symbol V represents an _ _ stroke.

An up-stroke should start on the lower side of the string and then proceed _ _ wards (away from the floor).

The symbol ⊓ represents a _ _ _ _ stroke.

An eighth-note (or quaver) has a duration of h _ _ f of a beat. It has a single flag attached to its stem.

Groups of eighth notes may be joined together with b _ _ m _ for ease of reading.

Complete the chart by filling in the gaps.

A bar in $\frac{4}{4}$ time has four beats

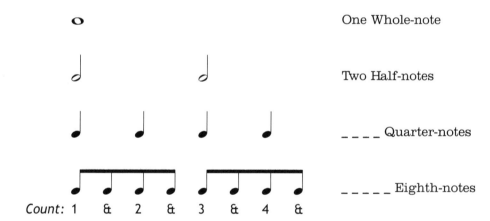

One Whole-note

Two Half-notes

_ _ _ _ Quarter-notes

_ _ _ _ _ Eighth-notes

Count: 1 & 2 & 3 & 4 &

Add the letter name for each note of the example shown below.

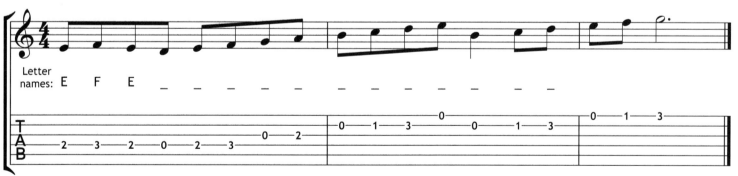

Letter names: E F E _ _ _ _ _ _ _ _ _ _ _ _

CHORDS

Complete the missing words.

Chord boxes are diagrams of the guitar n _ _ k viewed head upwards and face-on.

The two horizontal lines (one bold, one thin) shown at the top of the box represent the n _ _ .

The single horizontal lines represent the fr _ _ wir _ _ .

The vertical lines represent the str _ _ _ _ .

Complete the diagram of the chord box by labelling the strings with the correct letter names and fret numbers.

The numbered circles represent the position of your fi _ _ _ rs on the fretboard.

Open strings marked with an O should be played.

Open strings marked with an X should not be played.

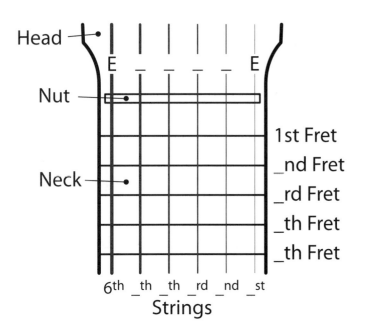

Complete the diagram of your left-hand fingers by filling-in the correct finger number (i.e. 1, 2, 3 and 4).

A chord may be represented above the music stave by a chord-sh _ _ _ which is often an abbreviation; for example: G Major is abbreviated to _ ; and G Seventh to _ _.

Draw as whole-notes (semibreves) on the stave, each note of the chord shown in the corresponding chord box. If you need some help, the Guitar Fretboard and Music Notation Chart (page 117) shows the relationship between the frets of the guitar and traditional music notation.

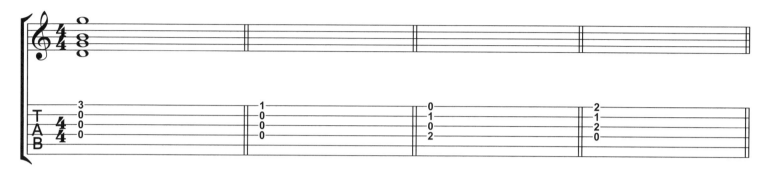

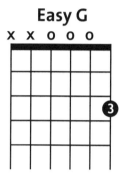

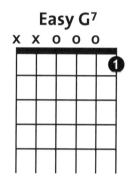

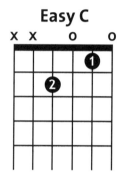

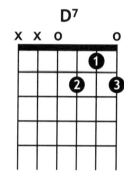

Rhythm slash notation is a convenient 'shorthand' way of suggesting the **rhy _ _ _** with which the chords may be **str_ _ _ _ d**. The stave has only one line because it doesn't need to show individual **n _ _ _ s**. The chord symbol tells you which chord to play and the chord box tells you which notes comprise the **ch _ _ _**.

A 'chord shape' is a 'shorthand' way of referring to the shape made by your **fin _ _ _ _** when they form a **ch _ _ _** .

Where no chord symbol is shown over a bar, play the chord shown in the previous bar.

When the notes of a chord are played in a 'staggered' way, they are called an **a _ _ _ ggio**.

5TH STRING QUIZ

Add the corresponding fret numbers for each note to the Tab stave and fill in their letter names on the spaces shown below.

Note _
Open
5th string

Note _
Second finger, 2nd fret
5th string

Note _
Third finger, 3rd fret
5th string

These three notes are too low to be placed on the stave so they are written on **le _ _ _ _** lines below it.

Add the letter names corresponding to each note.

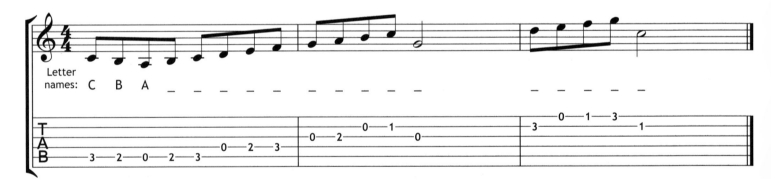

When describing 'minor' chords, arrangers tend to use a lowercase ' _ '. They tend to use a capital 'M' when describing _ _ **j** _ _ chords.

Complete the chord boxes by adding the appropriate left-hand finger numbers to the circles shown within them. Also, draw a '0' above each string to be 'played open' and an 'X' above each string which should not be played. The music stave below will help you remember.

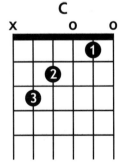

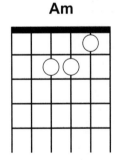

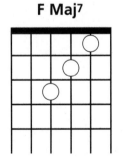

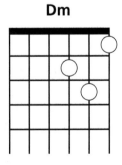

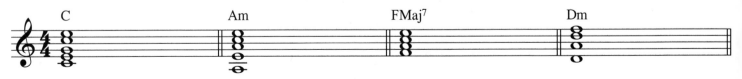

6TH STRING QUIZ

Add the corresponding fret numbers for each note to the Tab stave and fill in their letter names on the spaces shown below.

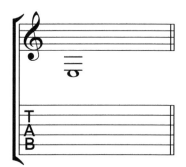

Note _
Open
1st string

Note _
First finger, 1st fret
1st string

Note _
Third finger, 3rd fret
1st string

Key Signatures

When it is known that (for instance) all the Fs will be sharpened in a piece of music, it makes sense to tell the musician at the beginning. This is done with a **k _ _ signature**.

The key signature for G Major takes the form of a **sh _ _ p** sign on the 'F' line (of the music stave) at the start of the piece.

Add the letter names to each of the notes shown below. Remember that the key signature raises all the F notes to F♯.

Occasionally a melody will start with an incomplete bar called an **a _ _ _ _ _ _ _ _** (or pick-up bar). The values of the notes missing from the anacrusis bar are added at the **e _ _** of the piece.

The symbol ♭ seen to the left of a note on the stave is called a **fl _ _** sign it lowers the pitch of a note by a **s _ m _ t _ n _** (or **o _ _** fret). The effect of a 'flat' ♭ symbol starts from where it appears in the bar and lasts until it is cancelled by the next **b _ _ line**. E♭ is pronounced E **fl _ _**.

When a flattened note is tied across a barline its effect lasts into the next bar.

Add the letter names corresponding to each note.

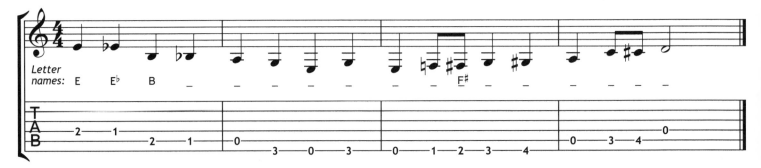

Letter names: E E♭ B _ _ _ _ _ _ _ F♯ _ _ _ _ _

Label all the notes in first position.

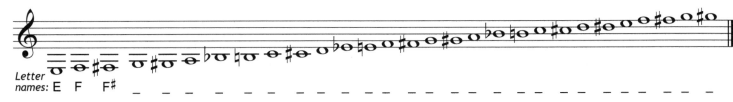

Letter names: E F F♯ _ _ _ _ _ _ _ _ _ _ _ _ _ _ _ _ _ _

GUITAR FRETBOARD & CORRESPONDING NOTATION CHART

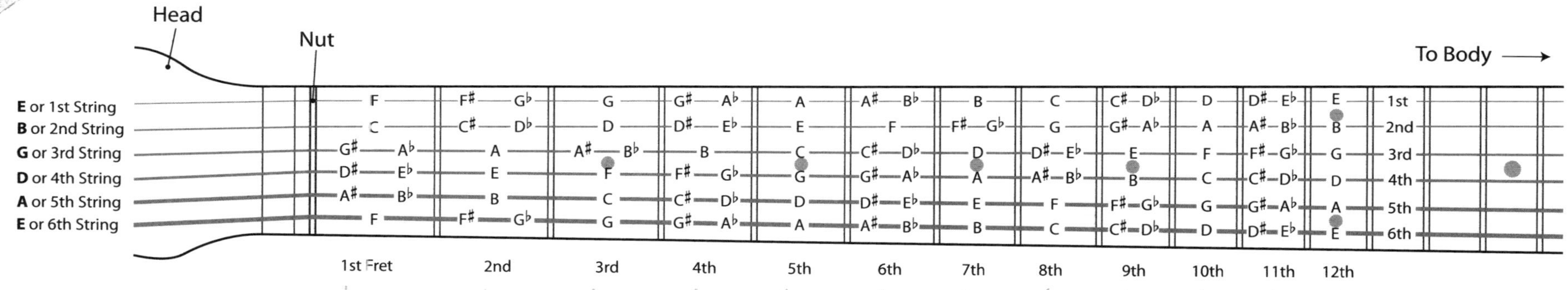
Head
Nut
To Body
E or 1st String
B or 2nd String
G or 3rd String
D or 4th String
A or 5th String
E or 6th String
1st Fret
2nd
3rd
4th
5th
6th
7th
8th
9th
10th
11th
12th
1st
2nd
3rd
4th
5th
6th

Open String
E or 1st String
B or 2nd String
G or 3rd String
D or 4th String
A or 5th String
E or 6th String

Sharps, Flats and Enharmonic Equivalents

All notes affected by an accidental may be 'spelled' either with a sharp or a flat. For example: D♯ (D sharp) is equivalent in pitch to E♭ (E flat), and A♯ is equivalent in pitch to B♭ etc… These are said to be enharmonic equivalents.

CD 1

CD 2

CREDITS

Published by:
Wise Publications, 14-15 Berners Street, London W1T 3LJ, UK.

Exclusive Distributors:
Music Sales Limited, Distribution Centre, Newmarket Road, Bury St Edmunds, Suffolk
IP33 3YB, UK.

Music Sales Corporation, 180 Madison Avenue, 24th Floor, New York, NY 10016, USA

Music Sales Pty Limited, Units 3-4, 17 Willfox St, Condell Park NSW, 2200, Australia.

Order No. AM990561
ISBN: 978-1-84772-083-2

Written by Rick Cardinali
Edited by Ann Barkway and Tom Farncombe
Additional editing by Scott Barnard
Guitar photos by iStockphoto and Shutterstock
Music processed by Paul Ewers Music Design
Designed by Paul Tippett, Adrian Andrews and Phil Russell for Vitamin P

All tracks created and recorded by Rick Cardinali
Additional production and engineering by Jonas Persson

Singers:
Rachel Lindley, Alexander Rhone and Tamara S

Backing Vocals:
Ann Barkway, Rachel Lindley and Jessica Williams

Musicians who contributed:
Ann Barkway, Rick Cardinali, Arthur Dick, Tom Farncombe, Johnny and the Stalkers
Mark Newby-Robson, Jonas Persson, John Rose

Printed in the EU

Your Guarantee of Quality
As publishers, we strive to produce every book to the highest commercial standards.

This book has been carefully designed to minimise awkward page turns and to make playing
from it a real pleasure.

Particular care has been given to specifying acid-free, neutral-sized paper made from pulps
which have not been elemental chlorine bleached. This pulp is from farmed sustainable forests
and was produced with special regard for the environment.

Throughout, the printing and binding have been planned to ensure a sturdy, attractive
publication which should give years of enjoyment.

If your copy fails to meet our high standards, please inform us and we will gladly replace it.

www.musicsales.com

1 2 3 4 5 6 7 8 9